Improving Our Acoustics for Hearing the Gospel

Reverend Frank Dew
With Jane Murden

Improving Our Acoustics for Hearing the Gospel
by Reverend Frank Dew & Jane Murden

Printed in the United States of America

ISBN 9781613796238

Illustrated by Lisa Mary Piatt

www.xulonpress.com

*To our spouses Michie and Frank
and to all those who help us
to hear the Gospel from the Street.*

*I*mproving *Our Acoustics for Hearing the Gospel* reflects the faithful work and life of the Reverend Frank Dew. Funny, challenging, and full of compassion, Frank draws us into the possibility of living the inward and outward journey of servant leadership. This is a call to action for all people of faith.

> Ruth Anderson, Executive Director of the Servant Leadership School in Greensboro, N.C.

(Frank and Jane) your heart for servant leadership, social justice, and ministry with the poor shines through this manuscript.

> Robin Pippin, Editorial Director, Upper Room Books

Thank you for sharing this (rewrite of an important chapter) with me. It's great. Your effort to be more inclusive paid off. I laughed when I read the 'PhD in life experiences' phrase because when I told Gordon (Cosby) that I'd suggested you try to work on this chapter he said, "Well, you know, lately I've been thinking in terms of some of us being school-trained and some of us being life trained. Some folks have earned higher degrees in life experience." So when I read this, I thought it was a good sign! You and Gordon being on the same wave length doesn't surprise me at all.

> Kayla McClurg from the Church of the Saviour in Washington, D.C.

Foreword/Introduction

T his book began on a retreat. I was giving a talk to a small group and my friend Jane Murden said to me, "You should write a book". With her encouragement and help, we began a conversation which became the text for this book. The outline of the chapters is largely a reflection of my experience with the Servant Leadership School at the Church of the Saviour in Washington, D.C. The movement from call to community to engaging the powers is the context for developing servant leaders that I learned from Gordon and Mary Cosby and others at the Church of the Saviour.

I have also reflected on my own experience of 30 years ministry, especially as Pastor of New Creation Community Church and as chaplain at the Greensboro Urban Ministry. This setting for ministry has given me the opportunity to be with the poor, the least, the last and the left out. This setting has helped me to hear the gospel in a way that seems more authentic and less theoretical.

My hope for this book is that it will serve as a basis for small group study and reflection which will encourage others to listen for God's call in their lives and to find concrete expression for what it looks like to follow Jesus.

Reverend Frank Dew

I met Frank Dew in 1985, we had just moved into our first home and he had just moved in next door. He had recently left a good job as solo head pastor of a large Presbyterian Church in Greensboro to start a church that would be really small and require true commitment from it's members, it was to be started in the fellowship hall of a church downtown. Since we were also Presbyterian I was somewhat interested but it sounded a little crazy to me.

We shared many years of neighborly comings and goings while raising children. Both families moved on, but always stayed in touch, aware of the others faith journey and sometimes joining together in certain activities like when Frank needed a Treasurer for a fledgling not-for-profit. Of course he called me, CPA's are always in demand. He explained that a few people wanted to start a house for mother's recovering from substance abuse where they could also live with their children. These people saw a need, even though there was not even one other program in the whole United States like they were envisioning. Hence I watched, while handling the money, the birthing of Mary's House. This was in 1998 or so.

In the spring of 2004 Frank and I found ourselves on a weekend retreat and enjoyed catching up. Frank gave a talk that weekend titled "Improving Our Acoustics". His talk really struck a cord in my heart and mind. I thought, 'Others really need to hear this'. Knowing that Frank was not just talking but had actually lived what he was saying in his talk, I went up to him afterwards and said, "We could make a book out of that sermon". That is how it started and we have been pushed and shoved along by the Holy Spirit ever since. We want to thank all the special friends that helped us along the way in encouragement, reviews and honest feedback.

My hope in helping write this book is to document for our generation and perhaps coming generations that Jesus Christ is alive at the turn of the 21st century. I have seen him in the life of my dear friend Frank Dew. By the telling of each other's stories we can see the Holy Spirit doing the work of the kingdom through fellow Christians. I also hope for myself and anyone who reads this simple work that they will not only be reminded of where Christ was and is but where each of us needs to be in order to hear His voice a little clearer. I definitely heard the call and hope you will too.

Jane Murden

Contents

Hearing the Call

"Immediately they left their nets and followed him."

The Word
The Calling of the First Disciples

Matthew 4:18-22

As he walked by the Sea of Galilee, he saw two brothers, Simon, who is called Peter, and Andrew his brother, casting a net into the sea - for they were fishermen.

And he said to them, "Follow me, and I will make you fish for people."

Immediately they left their nets and followed him.

As he went from there, he saw two other brothers, James son of Zebedee and his brother John, in the boat with their father Zebedee, mending their nets, and he called them. Immediately they left the boat and their father, and followed him.

It is not wise to think that the only way we can live for God is to become a minister or a missionary. Think how many people would be shut out from the opportunity to glorify God if this was true. Sisters and brothers in Christ, it is not the job but your earnestness; it is not your position, it is grace which allows us to glorify God. The name of Jesus can be glorified by the poor uneducated laborer and blesses God as much as the most popular preacher covered by national television. God is glorified by our serving Him in our given vocations. Be careful that you don't forsake your path of calling by leaving your occupation and also be careful not to dishonor your profession or occupation. Do not think that your calling is too little; you may be the only one able to reach those around you. Every lawful occupation can be sanctified for the noblest ends. Therefore do not be discontent with your calling. Whatever God has made your position, or your work, stay in it, unless you are quite sure he is calling you to something else. Let your first care be to glorify God to the best of your ability where you are.

paraphrased from "Morning and Evening: Daily Readings" by Charles Spurgeon

--------- One ---------

Hearing the Call

Call is what we do with our time, our soul and our stuff. Our talents have been given to us by God and God has a use for those talents.

Do we really want to hear?

Remember the song by Joan Osbourne, *What if God Was One of Us?* As I was thinking about that question it struck me that one of the questions many people would want to ask God would be, "What do you want me to be?" or "What do you want me to do?" To know the answers to those questions with certainty would be both very exciting and very scary. It would be so exciting to really know what God wants us to be and to do but also very scary to think, well, there's no getting around this! I know exactly what God wants me to be and to do. There would be no fudging or saying maybe this really isn't it. It is both exhilarating to think about knowing your call with such clarity but there is also a kind of burden associated with it.

It reminds me of when I went to my home pastor and I told him that I was thinking about going to seminary. He said, "Don't do it if you can do anything else." I thought, "Good grief, of course I could do something else! I'm not that bad off!" I really felt weird about his response at the time, but I came to realize what he meant. If you can talk yourself into doing something else then you really are not called to it. You may not want to do your chosen call every day but there is something about it that has a deep almost unexplainable hold on you.

Many people come to a point in their adult life when they say to themselves, "What am I doing here?' "Why am I doing this?" For me it was one Christmas Eve when I found myself conducting a funeral. It just seemed odd to be at such a sad event while my family was gathering for festivities. I then realized, even though I had made many choices along the way, that I had a real sense of being chosen. It is both exhilarating and a burden. As much as it felt that I was making choices, it was really God working God's purpose out in me and my life. Like Jesus said, "You did not choose me, but I chose you." We know that we make choices but we also come to the point when we look back and say, "Wow, God has been weaving God's purpose all along."

Call is something we are excited about, but also at a deeper level it has a hold on us. On those days when we say, "I don't really feel like doing this funeral today," or whatever needs to be done, you also have a sense that you can't really be satisfied if you're not doing it either. It is kind of like being in love. You don't necessarily like the person every day, but there is a commitment there and a deep connection that has a hold on you that you can't be satisfied without.

Call is what we do with our time, our soul and our stuff. Our talents have been given to us by God and God has a use for those talents. Our talents often lead us into the direction of our calling; however, sometimes God gifts us for a calling that God has in mind. In other words, sometimes we will find our call through our talents and sometimes God gifts us with talents that we need to have in order to do what God has in mind. Either way God is going to use our lives and our hands.

My call is different from anyone else's call and vice versa. What excites me is different from what excites others. I've got something in me that's chosen by God and I have chosen Christ, so the two together will be what God wants. As I choose Him, I come to realize more and more that He chose me first. I am living out of that 'choseness'. I'm choosing out of that 'choseness'. We each are made for our call.

Call Is for All

Call is not just for clergy. All followers of Jesus have a call to follow. Ministry is something every follower of Jesus is called to. The issue is what will be the form of your ministry. One of my friends is an accountant who struggled for years with the question, "How can an accountant be called?" One day a minister made the comment to her, "You can go into that business building and I can't." This comment awakened her to the fact that she was to be Christ's hands in the midst of her daily work as an accountant and that she would walk where "ministers" could not. She was able to see her fellow workers' pains and sufferings and lead them to where they could get help.

In addition, she was able to see that her work as an elder serving on the finance committee at her church was actually right where God wanted her to be. This led her to many different and exciting calls within the community as treasurer of non-profit organizations that needed her skills. God obviously had a plan.

One of my favorite call stories is from an interview with an older woman who had been a famous ballerina. As she was being interviewed they asked her to tell them about the early days, "Oh, gosh," she explained, "I used to work at so and so's washing dishes and so and so's waiting tables and in between those jobs I would go for rehearsals and tryouts." The interviewer says, "Wow, that must have been really tough juggling all that and just barely making a living," and the ballerina replied, "Yes, but I was dancing! That was what I was called to do. All of the stuff that enabled me to dance was nothing because it allowed me to do that one thing. All the practice, all the washing dishes, all the waiting tables was worth it because of that one thing."

Often a person cannot get paid to do what they have been called to do. Some of the most important calls don't result in pay. What you have to do is almost a "tentmaking" work, something on the side in order to make a living to be freed up to do what you are called to do. For example, in the Catholic tradition, people in religious orders may be teachers, social workers or nurses, doing work that is not incompatible with their call, but that allows them to live out their call of living a religious life. Monks might make cheese or wine in order to make a living which supports their community. Another example would be someone who owns his own plumbing business and uses his skills 'on the side' to help out on a Habitat project.

Called to greatness

Sometimes we have the idea that our call has to be some great thing that is written up in a book or on a billboard somewhere. Martin Luther King said, "Everyone can be great because everyone can serve." Jesus made it clear that greatness in God's kingdom is measured by servanthood. This reminds me of Mother Teresa's words, "We don't have to do great things but we can do small things with great love." A lot of what Mother Teresa did was like that—many small, daily acts done with great love.

Call is about being as well as doing. We often think of call as doing something. But I think it has both aspects. I know an older woman who went to seminary with a clear sense of calling to be a local pastor. When she completed her seminary degree, there was no calling from a local church. She was very disappointed and wondered what God was doing. Soon she received a call to serve as a chaplain for hospice. In the midst of this ministry she came to realize God's calling was not just about where she did ministry but how she did ministry. We are all called to greatness, but as defined by God when Jesus said, the first will be last....

God's call comes to us in many different ways

We would like it if we could figure out some kind of formula in order to know our call. We could just add up this column and that column and divide by two and it would tell us the answer, but God clearly does not work that way. When we look at the Bible we see a variety of call stories. Abraham and Sarah were too old, Jeremiah thought he was too young, Moses was confronted by a burning bush, Samuel and Isaiah were in the temple, Peter was by the sea shore, and Matthew was at the tax collector's table. Mary was a young woman, too young to be a mother, and Paul was persecuting the church when he was called. The point is, the Spirit blows where it wills.

One of the most helpful ways for us to discern our call is to watch other people respond to their call. It doesn't mean that I have to do it just like they do but seeing someone faithfully responding to their call helps me think that I can do that too. I may not do the same thing. But I can respond.

Listening for God's Call

The disciplines of prayer, Bible study and community fellowship can help us to be in a place where we can hear God's call. I remember during one Advent season I was running in the neighborhood near my home. As I began my run, I went by the Catholic Church and the bells from the steeple were playing Advent hymns. The farther away from the church I got, the less I was able to make out the melody of the hymns. This was like a parable to me of how our lives become disconnected from God and the noise of life covers over the sound of God's song when we move away from the church.

Often call feels very uncertain at first. There is that tug and gradually you find yourself doing what God wants you to do. As call begins to unfold, skepticism is natural and healthy. Yet at a deeper level you find that you couldn't do anything else. A call needs to be challenged and confirmed in your faith community. We don't get an email in Hebrew.

A call may come as a gradual dawning of God's purpose for our lives. It can involve an accelerating sense of inner direction. It can emerge through a gnawing feeling that we need to do a specific thing. On occasion, it can burst forth as a sudden awareness of a path that God would have us take.

Our calls are always evolving like a rose bud opening. If we are to respond, we need to listen, not only today but as today evolves into tomorrow. In times of transition, we need to listen with extra care. I have a friend, Hazel, who found herself alone at age 68, when her husband died, wondering why God had left her here. What plan could God possibly have? After several months of Bible reading, prayer and tears, asking God to give meaning to her life and promising to go anywhere and do anything God desired, a friend who had been to Yucatan, Mexico, on a medical mission team called requesting a visit. She told Hazel about a former Presbyterian mission in Mexico that needed someone who could cook and sew and be like a mother to the nursing students. Since Hazel was a home economist the work described was a perfect match for her. While her friend was talking, a peace settled over Hazel and she knew that was God's answer to her prayers. In that moment she felt her spirit responding to God's calling to go where God wanted her to go, even if that meant Mexico. For 25 years she spent two to three months each winter working in Mexico and during the summer months shared her story to help raise funds for the mission there.

Experiencing Resistance

Fear, ambivalence and cost are some ways I experience resistance. It's so ironic because I literally remember exactly where I was when I said I would never want to start a church from scratch. It was during my first divinity internship in Fayetteville, NC. I was working at Highland Presbyterian Church and my vision of ministry was all about the usual ladder-climbing career track within the established church. I was pretty sure that God had a wood-paneled office and country club membership for me. Little did I know what God's true plans were for my life.

I also remember where I was when I said, "You know, the Greensboro Urban Ministry (GUM) does great work, but I would never want to work there". The reason I said that was because I couldn't image working with alcoholics and drug addicts. The amazing thing has been that some of my greatest learning has been a result of participating in a number of 12-step groups in my work at GUM. As I look back on those experiences I know that it wasn't just about my choosing. Actually my denial of what I was being called to do was my first reaction.

Awareness of a call can actually cause us to feel resistance or inadequacy. Just as Moses argued with God, citing his own inadequacies and Mary, the mother of Jesus said, "How can I have a baby when I'm not even married?" we also may find ourselves questioning.

Focus and Freedom

Call does two things in our lives. It gives us focus for our lives and it also gives us freedom. Because we are called to this, we are free to say "no" to the other 99 things. So many people are over-extended and under-committed which means their lives are a mile wide but an inch deep; over-extended but under-committed. Call eliminates the over-extension, it stops us from trying to do everything and deepens our lives at the point of call. We focus on what our call is and our lives are organized around that. Therefore, we are free from the burden of the feeling that we have to do everything.

Tom Long, who teaches preaching at Emory University in Atlanta said, "To do nothing is to believe there is no God, to try to do everything is to believe that you are God, and to do what you can is to trust God with the rest." Focus on our call can free us from the burden of feeling like we must do it all. With the clarity of call, we are free then to do that which we are called to do and free not to try to do everything else.

Quotes from Gordon Cosby

As the Holy Spirit begins to lure us into the Body of Christ of which Jesus is the Head, uneasiness is normative because we've been called out of our comfort zone.

All of us had best find out what we really want to do and start doing it, with whatever it involves. If you have to give up your responsibility, give it up; if the church goes to pieces, so be it. But we must find out what we really want to do because nothing else is going to help anybody.

Notes:
What about this chapter spoke to you?
What difference could that make in your life?

——— Two ———

Communing with God

"Lord teach us to pray…"

The Word
Jesus' Teaching on Prayer

Luke 11:1-4

He was praying in a certain place, and after he had finished, one of his disciples said to him, "Lord, teach us to pray, just as John taught his disciples." He said to them, "When you pray say: Father, hallowed be your name. Your kingdom come. Give us each day our daily bread. And forgive us our sins, for we ourselves forgive everyone indebted to us. And do not bring us to the time of trial.

It is comforting to know that the disciples were also wondering about how to pray. All of us can do with some help just like they did. It seems that instinctively we want our own way and we try to manipulate God and bargain with him. We usually come to a place during our adult lives that we realize we could use some help on how to pray and what to pray for.

Jesus' disciples also felt like they did not know how to pray and they asked him to teach them. They wanted help just like we do because we desire a deeper relationship with God. Come let's encourage each other.

Art Simon (paraphrased from "Rediscovering the Lord's Prayer")

Communing with God

I cry aloud to God; I cry aloud, and he hears me.

Psalms 77:1

Our need of prayer

I think back on growing up in the church and hearing people use prayer as an excuse to do nothing. I remember hearing people discussing serious matters and it seemed to me that all too often they would say, "Well, I guess we will just have to pray about this." At that time, it sounded like another way of saying let's not do anything. This was in the context of my home church during the civil rights movement. People really did not want to do anything and so they would say, "Let us pray."

In more recent years I have come to realize that prayer *is* doing something. In fact, prayer should be the first thing we do. Prayer should also be the last thing we do. Everything we do should be done with prayer.

Prayer is about our relationship with God. That relationship begins in a vital way when we recognize our need of God. The most fundamental expression of prayer is, "God help me." We come to recognize our need of God. This can happen in all kinds of ways. It happens especially when we come up against something in life that we can't control or manipulate or when we can't create the outcome we want. That could be anything from a difficult course in school to a boyfriend-girlfriend issue, a broken family relationship, a difficult illness or the death of a loved one. It happens any-time we realize we are up against the limits of our abilities and we turn to God in our need and in our desperation. Then we pray for ourselves. It is like the old saying, "There are no atheists in foxholes."

When we are up against this type of situation in life; our relationship with God moves from the theoretical to the practical. We may not even know in a systematic way what we believe about God or prayer but we are moved to the action of prayer out of our need. We pray even when we don't know…it is above dogma. It's like: don't write me a book…do something!! That's when that relationship becomes vital. Don't hand me a book on how to change the tire! Come and fix it!!

In gratitude

The second kind of prayer I want to talk about is the prayer of gratitude. Out of our experience of need and our experience of God's grace, mercy and deliverance, we reach out to God. Prayer then becomes a thanksgiving. Praise the Lord! Thank God! Our whole outlook of appreciation for each day and each moment comes when we have experi-enced deliverance. Our deliverance helps us to be more aware of the gift of life. So when we find ourselves dealing with some particular mundane difficulty, e.g., I can't find a parking place and I'm ten minutes late for my meeting, we can fall back into that gracious realization that I am here! I have a meeting to go to! I have something meaningful in life that I can do! Thanks be to God!

I've been impressed with the gratitude expressed by people who have so little in terms of material possessions. It often seems that people who have very little are much more aware of what they have to be grateful for.

In a similar way I've known people with terminal illnesses who have a heightened awareness of the gift of each day. I don't want to wait until a doctor says you have cancer to appreciate the gift of each day and the opportunities to see God and to serve God. As some of my friends in twelve-step programs remind me, "Each day is a gift. That's why they call it the present."

My running partner and I were out early one morning. We were running in front of my house on a street that goes west to east. As the sun was coming up, I said, "Man, that's a beautiful sunrise." He said, "I've never seen an ugly one." That says it. That is gratitude. When you have that kind of outlook you can see the beauty around you and see God in all of creation.

For the World

In response to what God has done for us and in thanksgiving to God, we then pray for the world. We pray for the world because God loves the world. God sent his Son to the world, not to condemn the world, but to save it. We then become the intercessors for the world, lifting it up to God.

Intercessory prayer, like all prayer, is mysterious. I certainly do not have all the answers, but I do believe there is power in prayer. I don't know how to explain it or quantify it, but I believe there is power in prayer. I have seen it in action.

One example is when we (New Creation Community Church) first became concerned for South Africa during the 80's. An intractable situation existed in their country. Who would ever have thought that anything could happen to change apartheid? I remember one of my church members saying, "We need to pray." Part of my teenage years clicked in and I thought, "That sounds like doing nothing." However, we really did not do anything much but pray. In retrospect there was probably more power in the prayers than in all of the diplomatic efforts. It was prayer supporting all of the political activity that really made room for a miracle to happen, in terms of that transition and the barriers coming down, the end of apartheid in South Africa. Thanks be to God!

Another example was an ongoing prayer vigil in downtown Greensboro against the nuclear buildup during the Reagan years. When the Soviet Union fell apart the news coverage gave credit to the U.S. defense buildup as the cause of the breakup of the Soviet Union. I kept thinking, what about the prayers that were offered? The many, many prayers?

Again about three years ago, I began to think about the fact that we were executing people in our state and there was nothing being done about it. I went to my church members and said, "I think we should have a prayer vigil downtown." We started holding prayer vigils, just a small group of people, maybe ten, twelve, fifteen at the most. We faithfully met one day every month. A larger group started coming. We formed a local group: People of Faith against the Death Penalty. We took a resolution to the city council for a moratorium. The city council passed it. The state senate passed it. Who would have ever thought this would be possible! You couldn't even get anybody to have a meeting in a phone booth about the death penalty back before we started our prayer vigils.

Prayer not answered

There have been times I have prayed when I have not gotten the answers I wanted. This can be one of the most challenging times for our relationship with God. My 13-year-old nephew had cystic fibrosis and required a liver transplant.

We were all praying and praying. As a result of the surgery things went badly and he died of complications. I just could not understand it. Yet in the midst of that I believed that there was meaning and purpose that I couldn't see. The idea that kept coming back to me was from the passage in Romans about whether we live or whether we die, we are the Lord's. It wasn't that he was no longer in God's hands; he was still in God's hands. But I still did not understand the meaning of his illness and death.

In prayer we don't always get the answers we want. This does not mean that we should stop asking. This also doesn't mean that God isn't listening. God is listening. As we grow in our relationship with God, what we seek is more and more what God wants. What we desire is to become more trusting, believing there is meaning even when we don't see it. "Faith is the assurance of things hoped for; the conviction of things not seen" (Hebrews: 12:1-2).

Prayer from our center

The last type of prayer I'd like to talk about is centering prayer. Instead of praying for myself, thanking God or praying for the world, centering prayer is simply about being in the presence of God. It is being open to whatever God wants to give to me. Typically people think of prayer as our talking to God. Centering prayer is the balance of being open not only to what God may be saying to us, but also to how God is transforming us.

Over time centering prayer provides formation. One of the things I like about centering prayer is that you really don't have to do anything but show up. Just be there. Be present to God's Spirit. There is a lot of freedom in that. I don't have to be prepared. I don't have to have anything written down. I don't have to read anything. I just have to be...with God.

The analogy for me is standing in a nice warm shower. Often my best thoughts come to me in the shower and I'm just being there. So the image I have in centering prayer is that I am in God's presence and it is just like being in that nice warm shower, where I'm going to be until the hot water runs out. I'm just surrounded with God's grace. That's the way I think about it.

It's personal

Prayer in all forms is very personal. It is very hard to talk to somebody else about what God has done in your life without sounding like... "God's talking to me"...that there is some kind of weird thing going on. I remember a church leader who taught a series of classes based on the special moment when she felt as if God talked to her. She led the group into a spiritual discussion and built up to a point where she described herself watching geese on a lake some time after her husband had died. At that moment God opened her heart and she knew God was with her. The strange thing was that in the group she really focused on those geese instead of realizing that was just her moment; she was almost idolizing that moment and trying to share it with others and trying to make it into something grand for other people that it wasn't. That moment was for her. Exclusively. We are not to try to copy that moment and have everyone out looking at geese trying to duplicate that moment.

Perhaps, some of the different divisions within the church came from a unique experience that was a gift from God. People over time have tried to share those moments and even built doctrine around the experience. But God cannot be captured. The wind blows where it will.

We can share our story of faith, hope and experience but it is our story, just like in a twelve-step meeting. My story is not necessarily yours and yours is not necessarily mine. We each have a story to tell and we affirm each other by sharing and listening.

There's an old African proverb that says, no one can see the whole elephant. Each person has their own perspective on what they see. We can gather around the truth. I have my angle and you have your angle and we are looking at the same truth. I am not saying there are many truths. There is only one truth, but you have a perspective on it and I have a perspective on it. We are looking at the same thing. That is why the sharing of our stories is so important. We gather as the body of Christ around the truth.

Weakness in prayer life

Here is one of my problems with prayer. I am not good about praying by myself. I think it has something to do with my personality type. We have had times in our church where I would say to people, "Come at lunch and we will have a time of centering prayer in the parlor. Meet me there at noon on Wednesday." I needed to know that someone was going to be down there or I wouldn't do it. I would get down there and if no one showed up, I'd just go to lunch. I know better than that. But I don't do well left by myself. We all need to find out what it is that is keeping us from having centering prayer time. That is why my life is structured to help my prayer life.

I went on a retreat recently where we studied the enneagram. The enneagram is a geometric figure that maps out nine fundamental types of human nature and their complex interrelationships. It is a development of modern psychology that is rooted in spiritual wisdom and ancient traditions. The retreat helped me realize how each of us has different personality traits. We are all different and each one of us needs our own structure for our prayer life. I think that's important because for years I had felt deficient in my personal prayer life because I didn't do it well by myself. It wasn't a type of prayer that was the issue. It was the fact that I needed the accountability and community. In the enneagram I was the enthusiast. Well, if you don't have somebody to be enthusiastic with, it's no fun. If I'm there by myself, who am I going to get excited with? Approach prayer following your own personality traits and don't beat yourself up because you're not Thomas Merton or you're not Mother Teresa or some other great spiritual leader.

Let's do it

Prayer is actually the most important thing that we can do. It reminds me of the inward and outward dimensions of discipleship that The Church of the Saviour[1] talks about. If we are really praying we will be concerned about the world, and if we are really concerned about the world we will be praying for it. They go together.

I've come to appreciate that prayer is a discipline. It is something that we benefit from doing for its own sake. We need to pray. We cannot benefit as fully if we simply pick it up only when we feel like it. When it becomes a regular part of our lives we benefit from prayer. So gather your friends together if that is what you need. Spend time in nature if that is what you need. Go sit in a stained glass chapel if that is what you need. Whatever it is, just do it.

People are often afraid of becoming serious about prayer because it does take a time commitment. They are already so busy that they cannot image taking time out to pray. There is a part of me that wants to say, "Don't worry about that, just pray when you can." But that is not right either. It is true, yes, pray when you can. At least start somewhere. But those who are actually asking about prayer or how to pray are already being called to a further dimension of prayer life. Otherwise they wouldn't be asking. If someone is asking about prayer then it is my belief we need to tell them that it takes time.

You will need to practice it and make time for it. It would be just like saying to someone who says, "I want to get in good shape," and you respond, "It is going to take some time." We wouldn't say just exercise when you feel like it or when you can. That's not going to work. Likewise as a follower of Christ there are times when we would say, just pray when you can; because possibly at that moment in their life that is all the person can do. There can even be certain times in our lives when we feel like we can't pray. When we are hurt or in deep mourning; when our brains don't even seem to work for weeks—that is when we remember that Christ is praying for us and we can ask others to pray for us.

The time to develop the discipline of prayer is when we can pray and when we are striving. Then during the times in our lives when we are not able to set time aside, the prayer life we have had will sustain us. Just as call changes over time our prayer life will change over time. If we don't treat it as a discipline it is not going to get any stronger. So let's encourage each other to do it.

Power of prayer

I really like to keep in mind this quote from Karl Barth: "To clasp hands in prayer is the beginning of an uprising against the disorder of the world." That really brings together the activist and the contemplative spirit. It puts us in touch with the power that really can change things, which is God. That takes us back full circle to where we began which is our need. When we are up against the principalities and powers, things like the death penalty, apartheid, the oppression of nations and terrorism, we realize we are up against something much bigger than we are, but none of which is bigger than God. It is a way to connect the action with the contemplation. It plugs us into a power greater than ourselves. It helps us to be open to God's leading. It is at the point of our weakness that we are open to God's will. It is the experience of the weakness that opens me up to God's power and the realization of God's power. Out of that comes the gratitude for what God does. Then we can realize that only God can solve those problems, but in God's plan we are called to play a part.

Quotes from Gordon Cosby
    Christian faith involves a glad, joyful self-surrender. An awareness has dawned that the most wonderful thing in the world is simply, with all the stops out, to give one's life to a loving God.

    To be open to God is to be inevitably called into the cosmic purposes of God.

Notes:
What about this chapter spoke to you?
What difference could that make in your life?

Three

Listening in Community

*"Cast the net to the right side of the boat,
and you will find some."*

The Word
Jesus and the Miraculous Catch of Fish

John 21:4-6

Just after daybreak, Jesus stood on the beach; but the disciples did not know that it was Jesus. Jesus said to them, "Children, you have no fish, have you?" They answered him, "No." He said to them, "Cast the net to the right side of the boat, and you will find some." So they cast it, and now they were not able to haul it in because there were so many fish.

Sometimes we miss hearing the voice of God. The Holy Spirit gentle nudges us and we tend to ignore the whisperings of divine command and heavenly love. Our minds are closed. Events happen in our world that we should have seen and done something about but do nothing and therefore corruption makes headway unnoticed; good works that could have blossomed go untended.

We think about the price Jesus paid for our salvation and wonder. Even though he saw us as we would be; the unbelieving, backsliding, indifferent, careless, lax in prayer, and yet He said, "I am the Lord thy God, the Holy One of Israel, thy Savior...I have loved you. "

Please Holy Spirit, give us hearing ears and understanding hearts!

paraphrased from "Morning and Evening: Daily Readings"
by Charles Spurgeon

--------- **Three** ---------

Listening in Community

Look at those Christians and see how they love one another even when they don't agree with each other. How the world needs that kind of love!

Against the grain

S omeone once told me that an isolated Christian is a paralyzed Christian. The Christian life is meant to be lived out in community. In following Jesus we are trying to live a life that is counter-cultural, going upstream and against the grain. The Christian life is like trying to stay clean and sober in AA[2] terms. In order to live the Christian life we need a support group of people genuinely seeking to do something that is very difficult. Often when I find a person who claims they don't need community I believe what they are really saying is that they have found their values supported by the larger culture. They're not worried about being in a Christian community. They've got the support of the culture.

A community which is against the dominant consciousness, meaning against the grain of culture, is a necessary context for one who desires to become a new creation and put on the mind of Christ. You can't be that different by yourself. You're going to get flattened and molded into the dominant culture. Christian community has been the place where the Holy Spirit continues to breathe life into the church. It is the reason Christianity has survived all these years.

To live the Christian life in terms of following Jesus has always been counter-cultural. That's why from the beginning Jesus called together a group. It even goes beyond that. If we think about the very nature of God, the Trinity itself is a three-in-one. God's very nature is being in community. Therefore, I believe the purpose of creation is for God to be in relationship with others. Why did God create human beings? I think the answer is that God wanted to be in relationship with us and for us to be related to one another.

It can be hard

Of course the problem with community is that it is hard. I appreciate Gordon Cosby's[3] honesty about the difficulties and challenges of being in community. Community is not chosen by individuals, but given by God. As a result, we find ourselves with people that we would never have chosen and who would never have chosen us. People in community often experience bumping up against each other's fragilities, finiteness, and limitations. We experience those difficulties and we think that we have lost community. We experience problems and we say, "Oh my goodness, what happened to our community?" Scott Peck speaks to this in his book, *A Different Drum*. He talks about levels of community beginning with the surface level of a pseudo community, i.e., "How are you?" "Oh, I'm fine." "Are you fine?" "Well, that's just great." And that's all we ever do. Sometimes we get beyond that surface level and it's often because of difficulties we experience. Part of becoming real community is being willing to be vulnerable and to admit that there is some difficulty which forces us to take off our masks.

It reminds me of a time when we were meeting in a small group at our church. We had finished our study and our prayer concerns and we were about to pray and I said something like, "Does anyone have anything else to share?" A woman who was relatively new to our church spoke up softly and said, "I just want you all to know that I feel very alone." At that point her chin began to quiver and all of a sudden we were at a deeper level of community. Because she opened up and became vulnerable we were all at a deeper level. That's an example of how the sharing of our pain can often facilitate community. When we bump up against our own fragilities and limitations or the fragilities and limitations of others or when we experience people rubbing us the wrong way, we can either ignore it and keep our engagement at the surface level or we can go deeper in some way and confront it.

Scott Peck goes on to talk about moving from pseudo community to chaos where everything's a mess or where somebody's rocking the boat. At that point we often think we have lost community. But in fact this is a part of being community. It is much like family life. It isn't that you've lost your family, but that you are being family in the midst of difficulty. We call it dysfunctional. We think that we have lost functionality. Rather than staying with the conflict, we give up, resulting in broken families or communities. We think we have lost community, but in fact we are struggling through the conflict to become community at a new and deeper level.

By your love

Let's go back to what Jesus said, "By your love they will know you're my disciples." Not by your agreement, but by your love for each other. Sometimes we think that we all have to agree on everything. Paul uses the great image of the body. If one member is hurting then we are all hurting with them. If one member is celebrating, we are all celebrating with them. We are connected in that way. Every person, just as every part of the body, is necessary. There is a part for every person to play.

One of the beautiful things to me about the church is that we have this mandate to lift up the least among us. Those who are considered greatest in the world don't require as much attention in the church. Paul talks about this in terms of the least honorable parts of the body being given the greatest honor and the most honorable parts the least attention. Therefore, in the church someone with a physical handicap is cared for and ensured a place at the table. As the youngest, the oldest, the poorest, and the least educated are lifted up and cared for, we have done this unto Christ.

In the Quaker[4] tradition there seems to be an acceptance of individuality within the body. Quakers seem to know how to grapple with individual differences. They know that discussion and disagreement are part of being the body and that eventually consensus is needed for every decision. This requirement of consensus often means being willing to wait. We, as Presbyterians, have to say that it is time to vote. This can lead to winners and losers and if you don't like it, you can leave. That's when we break our community. I think the Quakers have a lot to show us with respect to building community.

One of the things that Paul talks about quite a bit is the importance of unity, because without unity the body cannot function. So we have to guard against splitting up the body. We wouldn't want our own bodies split up. But unfortunately we find it all too easy to split up the body of Christ, the church. We're fine about saying, "Well if you don't agree, you can go somewhere else." The biggest problem about that is the kind of witness that gives to the world. Again how does Jesus say they will know us? Not by our agreement but by our love for one another. Look at those Christians and see how they love one another even when they don't agree with each other. How the world needs that kind of love!

Chosen for community

Community is somewhat like a family in that you don't really choose your family. Neither do we really choose our church community. On the other hand, if you were going to join a club you would probably choose one made up of people more like yourself. Yet in my experience of church community, I find myself with people I never would have chosen. It is more of a commitment than a choice. It is a call that puts you in relationship with people that you never would have chosen. This diversity helps us to grow in ways that we would not if we were only with people who were similar to us.

I am talking about a community where you have heard from Christ the call to be in that community. Many people take the easy road. If they don't feel like they fit; they just don't stay, as if that were the only criterion. We need to be listening to the Holy Spirit in order to know if we are to stay in a specific community. We might say to God, "I don't like it here." And God might say, "Well, tough, this is where I am calling you to be." This goes against the grain of what is known in the church as the "church growth" movement. People who talk about how to grow churches often tell you that the way to grow churches is by gathering people who are alike; as you would grow a club or an organization. Members are encouraged to bring friends who are like them and who like them. Their basic approach is the idea that birds of a feather flock together. Thus you end up having churches that look like a particular demographic group, a particular type of bird. The problem with that is you don't have the diversity of perspective needed to help one another to grow and to see more of the truth.

What community requires

I found in a Campus Ministry newsletter a list of the following requirements for community: time, commitment, compassion, forgiveness, love, structured freedom and fun. I think that is a great list. All of those are important but I think time is the hardest one. I hear people talking about their desire for being in community but none of this can happen without time. I see so many people who just can't take the time for real community. One of the sayings we have at New Creation is that a community is not microwavable.

When you really get down to it there are lots of people who want the benefits of community but they're not willing to put in the time that is required. It really is required. It is just like in a marriage or any other relationship. You can talk all you want about quality time but if you don't have a certain quantity of time together you can't get to quality time.

I see people running around with all kinds of commitments, external commitments taking up their time, such that they are not able to experience community. The requirement of time has many dimensions to it. When we say we don't have enough time, it's time to listen for what it is that God is asking us to do. Where is God asking us to be? We must then have the courage, and ability to accept other people's criticism of how we are using our time. We have to accept that we will sometimes disappoint other people. Sometimes we will say "yes" and other times we will have to say "no."

We have to accept that we will not be able to do all the things we would like to do. We all have the time that God has given us. The question is, what are we doing with our time? Are we living out of our sense of call? Or are we living out of all of the other culturally determined needs that are calling us away from our true call?

It comes back to the notion of the urgent versus the ultimate. We're often pulled by the urgent. What do we have to do right now versus the ultimate things that give us peace, out of which we can live and operate and order our lives?

Discerning call

Throughout the history of the church, Christian community has been the place where individual calls must be confirmed. Through the affirmation of the community we experience whether or not it is just ourselves alone hearing this call. I think it is important to have a community where we can go with our struggle about call. There might be all kinds of issues in terms of blocks we are experiencing; various priorities and our other commitments in our lives. For example, a particular call may be in conflict with family needs or life situations. How does this call complement or conflict with our other commitments and how do we sort those out?

Paul had his individual experience on the road to Damascus but then he came back to the church at Jerusalem to work out his call to the Gentiles with his fellow Christ followers. There was not easy agreement concerning Paul's calling to the Gentiles and its implications. But Paul understood the necessity to come back to the church for its confirmation and blessing (Acts 11).

I can think of various times when we have helped members of our church to discern a call. I think of Miriam Bell, who felt a call to use her home in rural Guilford County as a small group retreat center[5]. She sounded that call at worship one night. She asked for folks to join with her in a mission group to further explore that call. The group came together and worked with her discerning how that call felt for her and how they could support her in pursuing the call. They listened with her and also felt the call and the need that would be fulfilled by it.

The question we can all ask of our fellow Christians is, "Do I have support for this call?" Within an honest, praying community you can get this feedback. Community can help confirm or deny call. I believe that the community will hear the Holy Spirit in the discernment process.

Waiting, experimenting, discerning

Gordon Cosby sounded a call for years about the Servant Leadership School in Washington D.C., but he did not get confirmation in terms of people being ready (or called) to join him in that call. So for years he waited. He did not proceed until other people started to be called. Our waiting is purposeful also. I think the waiting honors community. It is saying I cannot do this by myself. God is not asking us to do our call by ourselves. It wasn't that Gordon Cosby didn't feel that the call was real, but the timing was not right. He was waiting for God's timing, which can feel like giving up or doing nothing.

A minister friend and I were talking about call. He had an experience where a church member really felt like he was being called to youth ministry. The person was given an opportunity to try that call out within the church. Part of call is experimenting to see how it goes and to experience the fruits. In this particular situation the person did not relate well with the youth. Because he did not have the communication skills to relate to kids, he was turning some of the kids off.

As a community, then, it is also our responsibility to say we don't think this is your call, pointing out some of the fruits, but being sure to do it in love. That is a hard thing to do because, we are afraid someone might not like us or is going to feel bad. Working through each other's call is a part of building community, and building community is one of the hardest tasks.

Moving on

God may be calling us to stay right where we are and sometimes we are called to leave a certain community. That is a hard thing. As pastor of New Creation Community Church, when others have moved on, it has been hard because I love them and I love this community. I'm the kind of person who thinks everyone should love it just as I do. But I've had to realize that's not the case. This particular community is not where everybody belongs, but so far it is where I belong.

I remember that when we first started New Creation, Gordon Cosby said, "You know this is not for everybody." I wondered how that could be. Because it is so right for me, I thought everybody should want it. But I've had to realize it is not for everyone. That doesn't make us wrong nor does it make them wrong. It is just not for everyone. There are times when it is appropriate for people to come into a community and for them to leave. I think that has to do with call. When someone leaves a community, the ones who are left often experience a sense of loss. There is a grieving process that we have to admit and accept, allowing a time for grief without bitterness. As a pastor, it is hard when people leave a community. However, I don't want to be the kind of pastor who's trying to hold on to people for the sake of holding on. The point should be to help people to grow in hearing God's call in their lives and to respond to it.

Quotes from Gordon Cosby

I think the freer a person is inwardly, the more deeply rooted in Christ the community is, the easier the structures can change to meet new times. God is always doing new things.

I believe that the only hope of the world is the existence of Christian communities which are completely real, in which there is no artificiality, no equivocation.

Notes:
What about this chapter spoke to you?
What difference could that make in your life?

Being with the Poor: A Spiritual Discipline

*"Then he put him on his own animal,
brought him to an inn, and took care of him."*

The Word
The Parable of the Good Samaritan

Luke 10:29-37

But wanting to justify himself, he asked Jesus, "And who is my neighbor?"

Jesus replied, "A man was going down from Jerusalem to Jericho, and fell into the hands of robbers, who stripped him, beat him, and went away, leaving him half dead.

Now by chance a priest was going down that road; and when he saw him, he passed by on the other side. So likewise a Levite, when he came to the place and saw him, passed by on the other side. But a Samaritan while traveling came near him; and when he saw him, he was moved with pity.

He went to him and bandaged his wounds, having poured oil and wine on them. Then he put him on his own animal, brought him to an inn, and took care of him. The next day he took out two denarii, gave them to the innkeeper, and said, "Take care of him; and when I come back, I will repay you whatever more you spend."

Which of these three, do you think, was a neighbor to the man who fell into the hands of robbers?"

He said, "The one who showed him mercy."

Jesus said to him, "Go and do likewise."

Christian life has a stream of social justice within the faith that calls forth justice for all human relationships and social structures. Jesus gathered all the laws and put them into two; to love God and to love our neighbors. They stand as separate commandments but actually the love of God drives us to compassionate love of neighbor.

Social justice brings harmony to relationships between people. We care for each other and learn to appreciate each other. We are made in the image of God and are therefore infinitely precious beings. When we learn to hear and respect people of other cultures and develop true friendship with them we become wiser people. Working for social justice can teach us that we can be diverse and still live as one within Christ.

paraphrased from "Streams of Living Water"
by Richard Foster

———— **Four** ————

Being with the Poor:
A Spiritual Discipline

"Whoever is thirsty should come to me, and whoever believes in me should drink. As the scripture says, 'Streams of life-giving water will pour out from his side.'" John 7:37-38

Recognizing need

When we talk about being with the poor, it is important to talk first of all about what it means to be poor. In Luke's gospel, we find Jesus speaking about, "Blessed are the poor...". Here I believe Jesus was speaking about the economically poor, those lacking in material things of food, clothing and shelter. In Matthew's gospel, we find Jesus speaking about, "Blessed are the poor in spirit..." and in this case, I believe Jesus' words are referring to people who are in need in a broader sense. Those who are "poor in spirit" reflect people who are up against situations in life that they cannot change, cure or control. Both "the poor" and "the poor in spirit" are people who are left out by the mainstream of society. They are the marginalized who are the least, last and left out in our world. Examples of "the poor" and "the poor in spirit" range from a hungry child in India to a person addicted to drugs in the United States to a lonely teenager anywhere. Whether we are "poor" or "poor in spirit," when we are forced to recognize our own need, then we are more able to acknowledge our need of a savior.

When we first began New Creation Community, one of the first things we decided was that we wanted to have a connection with "the poor." And so we began by providing breakfast and worship at the Greensboro Urban Ministry night shelter one Sunday morning every other month. This was obviously not a large commitment, but it was a beginning. After providing breakfast and worship for several months, I was feeling very righteous. I felt like we were doing what Jesus would have us do. But after several more months, one of our members came to me and said, "I don't feel like I am getting to know any of these people. I don't feel like I am really getting to know their names and their stories." Well, there she had gone and rained on my parade. But she was right. Here we were, sharing breakfast and worship together and yet we were not really connecting. Why?

What I realized was that I had seen this whole experience as a one way transaction. We were there providing breakfast and worship, but because of my own prejudices I could not see anything that these "homeless" people had to give to me. Because we so often judge someone's worth based on their financial well being, I was not able to see folks who were "homeless" as people who had anything to give to me.

With heads bowed

Another experience that helped me to see more clearly came from our desire at New Creation to help support a Presbyterian Church (U.S.A.) missionary. We had a special interest in Nicaragua because of our government's support for the contras in that nation. We were blessed to be able to assist in the support of two P.C. (U.S.A.) missionaries in Nicaragua, Chess and Gay Campbell. Through our connections with Chess and Gay, we were able to visit them in Nicaragua. While we were with them, I remember in particular listening to a peasant farmer being translated from Spanish into English as he spoke about his life experiences. I remember thinking, here I am far away from home listening to this poor farmer and I am taking notes like I am in a college class. Then it occurred to me this poor farmer has a Ph.D. in life experiences that I don't have. He had so much to give to me that I had not seen before. My eyes were opened in a new way. Now, I realized there were people back home in Greensboro who had Ph.D.'s in life experiences that I did not have. They had so much to teach me.

About this same time I read an article by Ernest Campbell entitled "Believing in Christ or Following Jesus." In this article, Campbell talks about our ability to separate our "belief" in the second person of the Trinity from our willingness to follow the example of Jesus. He said, "If I am following Jesus, why is it, when I have finished with my giving, that I have so much left over for myself?" In another part of the article Campbell goes on to ask, "If I am following Jesus, why do I have so many friends among the affluent, and so few among the poor?" If I am following Donald Trump, it might make sense. But, if I am following Jesus, going to the places he went, reaching out to them I must ask myself why do I have so many friends among the affluent and so few among the poor?

We all know who friends are. They are people whose names and stories we know. They are people I enjoy spending time with. I had to ask myself, who are the people I hang out with?

At this point I began to hear a real calling to be with the poor. This came in the form of the recognition of a need to develop a chaplaincy program at the Greensboro Urban

Ministry. I went to the Reverend Mike Aiken, the Executive Director of the Greensboro Urban Ministry (Mike and I had been friends in college and seminary together) to share with him my idea. I said the Urban Ministry has programs to help people with food, clothing, financial assistance and housing, but there is no intentional program to help people put their lives together spiritually. Mike was very supportive of the idea and before long I found myself working part-time as the chaplain at the Greensboro Urban Ministry. One of the first things that we did was to begin to hold worship services each day at 12:30p.m.

After several weeks, I began to notice that many of our homeless guests and clients would begin their prayers by saying, "Thank you, Lord, for waking me up this morning." After hearing this prayer over and over again, I began to realize I had assumed that I would wake up the next morning. But, if I had spent the night sleeping underneath a bridge, not knowing who might walk by or what might happen, I too might begin my prayer by saying, "Thank you, Lord for waking me up this morning."

Another thing that I noticed at the Urban Ministry, in our Potter's House soup kitchen was how often people took the time to bow their heads and give thanks when they were about to eat. I thought about the many times when I had been in upscale restaurants and not seen any heads bowed in thanks. There was just something about people who seemed to have so little, and yet, so often they were teaching me through their gratitude how much they had. People who were poor and homeless had lost so much that it seemed there was less room for pretense.

When I was growing up, I can remember watching the local news covering a fire in a poor section of town. The local newscaster was there with a woman whose house was ablaze and the newscaster said, "What are you going to do?" and I can remember the woman saying, "I guess I'll just have to depend on the Lord." Whereas if they had come to my house and it was on fire, I probably would have said, "Thank God, it was insured!"

Along the roadside

My economic situation can insulate me from the reality of my dependence on God. The truth is, we all depend on God no matter whether we sleep under a bridge or under a canopy bed. It has also been my experience in working with the poor that for the most part, there is less pretense at a homeless shelter. There is less need to cover up the many losses that homeless people have experienced. The opportunity is there to get real and to be honest, without playing a lot of games and without the pretense of being fine, when none of us is really fine. There is something about being with the least, the last and the left out of our society that helps improve the acoustics for hearing the gospel.

It may seem strange to say, but being with the poor has helped me to see my own poverty and my own need of God. One such experience happened when a friend invited me to the AA meeting where he would pick up his twelve-year chip. The meeting began with everyone introducing themselves, "Hi, I'm Bob (or whatever their name was). I am a recovering alcoholic." When it came time for me to introduce myself, I wanted to say I was an alcoholic just to fit in, but instead I said, "Hi, I am Frank. I am a recovering sinner." Well, I got a big laugh, but more importantly, it was true. I was able to hear more clearly in that group my own need for a savior.

In the story of the Good Samaritan, we often see ourselves in the role of the Good Samaritan or perhaps one of the passersby, but rarely do we see ourselves as the beaten bloody body along the roadside in need of saving. Being with the poor has helped me to see myself as not just the giver, but also the receiver, the one in need of help. I have come to see that there are many more things in this life than I realized that I can't change, cure or control. And this has helped me to hear the good news of God's saving grace in Jesus as being also for me. Seeing more clearly my own need of God's grace and mercy has helped me also to recognize rich or poor, marginalized or mainstream we are all neighbors.

Voluntary poverty

I want to conclude this chapter on 'Being with the poor' by talking about voluntary poverty. This is a poverty that is chosen, not imposed. It is poverty that leads to a solidarity, an inclusivity and a mutuality that is freeing. For me, St. Francis of Assisi is a model of such voluntary poverty. Francis experienced a conversion that led him from a life of privilege to a life of poverty. Throughout Francis' life of poverty, he continued to experience conversions which resulted in greater and greater freedom from things and greater and greater dependence on God. The result was, less meant more. For us to, less materially means more spiritually.

Practically speaking, I believe that just as Francis was called to rebuild the church, so too are we called in our day to follow his example of voluntary poverty. This will lead us to rebuild and renew the church in a way that recognizes that we all stand in need around the Lord's table of grace and each one of us has a perspective from our life experiences which allows us to share with others. In this way, when we find ourselves beaten and in the ditch, we allow Jesus to save us through each other. We become neighbors regardless of wealth or poverty at the table.

Quotes from Gordon Cosby

God is the descending God. The movement is down, down, down, until it finds the sickest, the most afflicted, the most helpless, the most alienated, the most cut off.

I think one of the most serious things which can ever happen to a person is not knowing whether anyone has ever cared to know what was going on in their life.

Find a few poor (marginalized) people and spend some quality time with them.

Notes:
What about this chapter spoke to you?
What difference could that make in your life?

──────── Five ────────

Within New Creation
Community Church

"...In Christ, God was reconciling the world to Himself."

The Word

2 Corinthians 5: 16-20

From now on, therefore, we regard no one from a human point of view; even though we once knew Christ from a human point of view, we know him no longer in that way.

So, if anyone is in Christ, there is a new creation: everything old has passed away; see everything has become new!

All this is from God, who reconciled us to himself through Christ, and has given us the ministry of reconciliation; that is, in Christ God was reconciling the world to himself, not counting their trespasses against them, and entrusting the message of reconciliation to us.

So we are ambassadors for Christ, since God is making his appeal through us; we entreat you on behalf of Christ, be reconciled to God.

Unison Corporate Prayer

Gracious God, you call us, your church, to be the body of Christ, touching, healing, renewing, restoring. Yet as a body, we often fail to be fully connected. Sometimes we permit our problems to disrupt our community; the foot is a long way from the ear, yet both are needed if we are to hear the music and dance. Sometimes we permit differences to divide us; the right hand is good at reaching to the right and the left hand at stretching to the left, but both are needed to grasp the kingdom. Sometimes we are too disconnected to feel one another's hurts; but a kidney stone is not a localized problem, the pain of that small organ affects the whole body. And sometimes, as a result of our sin, tongues grow sharp and hearts grow hard, and arms fail to embrace. Forgive us our too small, too localized, too self-centered vision of what Christ's body should be. Help us to remember what we are called to be. Teach us community, O God, Kingdom Community that is real and radical, for without it we cannot hope to embody the presence of Christ, in whose name we pray. Amen

New Creation Community Presbyterian Church
October 28, 2007

Within New Creation Community Church

There has to be a certain amount of personal sacrifice in order to have community. We have to give up something in order to receive something. We have to empty ourselves in order to be filled. This is how community works.

In the Beginning

I've always had a kind of love hate relationship with the church. I've loved the church. I've felt at home in the church. I've grown up in the church and I'm grateful for the church. At the same time, because I have such a love for the church, I get so disappointed when the church isn't all that it could or should be. Because of that I've always had this yearning to be a part of a congregation that was authentically trying to be what the church could be and doing the things the church could do.

I felt a calling to begin a new congregation based on my experiences with Presbyterian Pilgrimage and The Church of the Saviour in Washington, D.C. The Pilgrimage experience gave me a sense of what Christian community could really be like, i.e., it could be at a deeper level than, "How are you doing?" "Oh I'm doing fine." "You're fine?" "Oh, yes, we're all fine." But none of us are really fine. We are just keeping it on the surface level. The Pilgrimage weekend, in particular, gave me an experience of what Christian community could be with many people I never had known before.

The other experience was with The Church of the Saviour. At The Church of the Saviour what really spoke to me was the way they put together the idea of an inward and outward journey. Following Jesus has these two dimensions of growing in relationship with God and being sent out into the world in service, all based on a sense of God's call in your life. That call to ministry was something that was shared in the community of faith. It wasn't something done by the pastor and everyone showed up on Sunday to hear or see what the pastor was doing. The community of faith was truly a priesthood of all believers caring for each other and being sent out for service in the world. Something within me said, "I've got to try this." I just knew if I never tried it I would be 65 years old and saying, "Oh no, I just did the typical thing."

I wanted the new church to be within my own denomination (Presbyterian Church USA) because I didn't want people to be able to easily dismiss it as some crazy group. I also really felt that our denomination needed something new. Just as we have hospitals responding to people's needs in established ways, we also needed a congregation where research and development could be done, where new patterns could be developed without leaving the orthodox theology, and where a new way of living out the Christian life could be explored. Actually, I believe our basic theology is sound. What we wanted to do was to connect what was in our minds to our hearts and then to our feet. We need greater opportunities to experience God and then to follow in the way of Jesus.

Two or More Gathered

The choosing of a name for a new church was a new experience in itself. I had already begun to fantasize about a name; like naming a new baby. I also knew that this had to be a process that would involve the whole community. Clearly that would be important. As we began to talk together, the name New Creation Community began to emerge. It was not a name that I had thought of before. This was a real experience in community for me. I realized that community means being able to let go of my agenda in order to take hold of a shared agenda which was much better than anything I could have come up with on my own. This is an important aspect of community. There has to be a certain amount of personal sacrifice in order to have community. We have to give up something in order to receive something. We have to empty ourselves in order to be filled. This is how community works.

As a result the sum is greater than the individual parts. When we are willing to empty ourselves, God can fill us. In letting go, we actually experience that there is more here than each of us or even all of us. Where two or three are gathered in Christ's name, there is a new creation. This could be said of any church. A church is a community of people who are being made new in Christ.

Acts, Chapter 2, where it describes the life of the early church provides a good blueprint for our life together. They prayed together. They worshipped together. They broke bread together. When anyone was found to be in need, they gave what they had. I saw this blueprint reflected in the tripod of Presbyterian Pilgrimage: piety, study, and action. As a result, we organized our life together around worship, nurture, and witness. We have four elders: one for worship, one for nurture, one for witness, and one for administration.

Worship

From the beginning, we wanted our worship to be central to our life together. Also, from the earliest days, we knew that we wanted to have communion every Sunday. This goes back to the fact that John Calvin wanted the church in Geneva to have the Lord's Supper each Sunday. Many of our early members had also experienced daily communion on the Pilgrimage weekend and found this meaningful. We also wanted to have a shared meal as a part of worship. Having a meal together provided a real opportunity for fellowship as opposed to people just filing out the door, saying "good sermon, good sermon, good sermon."

The style of music, communion service and the eating together were all centered around becoming a Christian community. The worship was very participatory. This involved the use of lay worship leaders and congregational participation in singing, announcements, and prayers. The music involved a variety of styles, including contemporary, gospel, traditional and Taize. Our hope was to draw closer to God and to each other as we worshipped together.

Study

We also began to study in small groups, using the same materials throughout the church to draw us closer as a community. We quickly realized that if we were to be growing in our faith, we had to be getting new input. This meant that we wanted to find a way to deepen our understanding of what our faith was all about. This required us to study the Bible, theology, ethics, church history and spiritual practices. We also had to learn to connect what we heard with our heads to our hearts and to our lives.

Witness—Intentional Connection

For New Creation Community, witness has been a very important and distinctive piece. For example, during our first year the Synod of North Carolina (PCUSA) passed a resolution against apartheid in South Africa. The resolution said that there would be a vigil at the South African embassy in Washington, D.C. Our church was the only one in Greensboro to participate in the vigil. We took about 12 people from our 40-person church to Washington, D.C., which became a precursor of things to come. This later led to our sponsoring Ali and Kefilwe, two black Presbyterian South African students, to go to college at the University of NC at Greensboro. We have since visited South Africa and continue to stay in contact with them.

Another thing that happened early on was participation in mission work in the Yucatan of Mexico. This was a response to Hazel Clawson's call. This also led to our desire to help support Presbyterian mission work. At that time the U.S.-sponsored contra war was ending in Nicaragua. We asked about Presbyterian mission work in Nicaragua and learned that Chess and Gary Campbell were missionaries in Managua. When they were in the U.S. they came and preached at our church. They said, "Why don't you come down and see what we are doing?" which we did. As a result of our trip, we began a sister church relationship with the San Pablo church, the first Christian Base Community in Nicaragua. This was part of the liberation theology movement in the Catholic Church in Latin America.

This sister church relationship has taught us a great deal about partnership and development. Ten of us spent a week with them, and two years later, we raised the money for 10 of them to visit us. We have also exchanged letters that resemble epistles. In addition, we have assigned prayer partners to all of our members. Our goal is a true partnership that helps us each to see the gospel and the world more clearly from another's perspective. This means that our mission is more about building relationships than anything else. Barbara Clawson and Anne and Charlie McKee, based on their inter-relational

85

experiences in Africa and Latin America, have really helped us to see our neighbors far away as partners on the way of learning what it means to follow Jesus.

Also, from the beginning there was a desire at New Creation to have an intentional connection with the poor in our local community. This led us to serve breakfast and provide worship at the Urban Ministry. Our experience with neighbors far away helped us to see neighbors nearby also as friends who can help us to see the way of Jesus more clearly. This connection has led to more homeless people worshiping with us. We have grown and continue to grow into a more diverse congregation socio-economically and racially. This has been exciting, but also very challenging at the same time. While diversity has been a blessing, it is not always easy to live with. Based on our background and experience, many of us find it hard to be a true friend to someone who is different. The person who has a lot of stuff feels guilty about having so much compared to another person. The person who has very little may be worried that the other person will think less of them because they have less. As we worship together, we believe these barriers can be broken down. Our growing diversity has been a blessing that has allowed us to hear and to see the hand of God at work in new ways. Our worship experiences have led to friendships which allowed us to hear a call to begin a halfway house for women coming out of substance abuse treatment and their children. Mary's House, the outcome of this call, was another example of listening for and hearing God's call in community.

Finally, one more example of call leading us in our witness has come from Ginnie Tate's call to begin a community garden. This garden has allowed us to share its produce and to witness to the importance of caring for the creation around us.

At New Creation, we don't want to just "talk the talk." We want to "walk the walk," and our witness life gives us an opportunity to do just that. As a new church, we were eager to listen for God's call and to go where God wanted us to go. And it helped that we had very little to lose, and therefore, we were free to follow God's call. I pray that this will continue to be a part of our identity.

Created to Follow

If we simply work on a cause without following Christ, we simply witness to the current culture and satisfy our own concerns and ego. We look for rewards from friends and family or even just society to recognize us 'good' people.

As we look to God and follow Christ we do this with fellow believers. We worship, study and take action together in order to witness for Christ. As we take action, our desire is to follow Christ. Our desire is to go where He would go, serve those who He would serve in today's society.

Quotes from Gordon Cosby

To me it is obvious that we should reduce our physical security needs and transmute those needs to deeper needs: the need for silence, the need for love, the need for friendship, and the need for serving others.

Christ is calling us to a lifetime of belonging.

Notes:
What about this chapter spoke to you?
What difference could that make in your life?

Within All Believers

*"Come you that our blessed by my Father,
inherit the kingdom prepared for you from the
foundation of the world."*

The Word
The Sheep and the Goats

Matthew 25:31- 40

"When the Son of Man comes in his glory, and all the angels with him, then he will sit on the throne of his glory. All the nations will be gathered before him, and he will separate people one from another as a shepherd separates the sheep from the goats, and he will put the sheep at his right hand and the goats at the left.

Then the king will say to those at his right hand, 'Come, you that are blessed by my Father, inherit the kingdom prepared for you from the foundation of the world; for I was hungry and you gave me food, I was thirsty and you gave me something to drink, I was a stranger and you welcomed me, I was naked and you gave me clothing, I was sick and you took care of me, I was in prison and you visited me.'

Then the righteous will answer him, 'Lord, when was it that we saw you hungry and gave you food, or thirsty and gave you something to drink? And when was it that we saw you a stranger and welcomed you, or naked and gave you clothing? And when was it that we saw you sick or in prison and visited you?'

And the king will answer them, "Truly I tell you, just as you did it to one of the least of these, who are members of my family, you did it to me.'

The Apostles' Creed

I believe in God the Father Almighty, Maker of heaven and earth;

And in Jesus Christ his only Son our Lord; who was conceived by the Holy Ghost, born of the Virgin Mary, suffered under Pontius Pilate, was crucified, dead, and buried; He descended into hell; the third day He rose again from the dead; He ascended into heaven, and sitteth on the right hand of God the Father Almighty; from thence He shall come to judge the quick and the dead.

I believe in the Holy Ghost; the holy Catholic Church; the communion of saints; the forgiveness of sins; the resurrection of the body; and the life everlasting. Amen

Within All Believers

*Be like new born babies, always thirsty for the spiritual milk,
so that by drinking it you may grow up and be saved. As the
scripture says, "You have found out for yourselves how kind
the Lord is."*

1 Peter 1:2-3.

The leading of the Spirit

"The church reformed and always being reformed"
is an expression that came out of the reformation
expressing the idea that the church is a living body filled
by the Spirit always becoming new. We as Presbyterians
come out of the reformed tradition. I have often heard this
phrase used as if it were past tense and was something that
happened back in John Calvin's day and then it was done
and over with. Actually, the reformers were talking about
the Spirit which gives life to the church and continues to do
so. This means the church as the body is constantly being
remade, reanimated and recreated. Therefore, I think it is
very important for the church to be open and discerning
about the leading of the Spirit.

One of the things that concerns me is that many churches today, especially in North America, are being driven by a concern for survival. Success is measured in terms of things; like number of members and money in the offering plate, size of the building or parking lots. I also get concerned about how the church seems to be adopting a business model and evangelism is being replaced by marketing concepts. Some worship spaces, in fact, look more like T.V. studios where you have an audience and performers creating entertainment as opposed to worship. This approach attracts performers to the stage and turns the congregation into the audience.

All too often, in the church, we are prone to segmenting and compartmentalizing our lives. For example, people come to church and hear about the Sermon on the Mount and "love your enemies," and think that is great. Then, all of a sudden there is a crisis in the world and the Sermon on the Mount goes out the window in favor of national security. All that talk about "love your enemies" fades away and we are living out of a whole different set of values. This is a huge challenge for the church, as we try to speak truth to those in power when we are so much a part of the powerful. When push comes to shove, we are tempted to throw out Jesus in the interest of trying to protect our "way of life." Of course on a deeper level Christ is (or should be) our life.

Falling short

Because poor marginalized people don't have any missiles or insurance to turn to, they more quickly turn to God. We who are more affluent have more options. We have the option to turn away from God to find our source of security elsewhere. We have the illusion of being in control. Throughout history there has been this pull in the direction of compartmentalizing our lives so that we live out of different sets of values in different settings. We live out of one set of values at work, and then we come home and live out of a different set of values. Then we go to church and live out of a different set of values. The challenge for the church is to help us to live out of the values of Jesus no matter where we are in all the places of our lives. Living out the Christian life is a daily challenge.

As we move closer to integrating the values of Jesus into all aspects of our lives we will have a more effective witness. Not that we will ever do it perfectly, but we are trying to put all of life under the umbrella of God's kingdom. That is what the world needs to see and what we as Christians need to demonstrate as opposed to some new bumper stickers or billboards or a new and improved marketing strategy. Leaving Christ out of the equation may lead to a successful human institution, but it will be devoid of the power to change lives. The truth is that most successful human institutions tend to reflect the culture rather than transform it. What is marketing strategy anyway but finding out what the people want and giving it to them. The gospel on the other hand recognizes what people need and meets people at the point of that need.

Trusting God with the outcome

These are important issues because in the church today, so much of what is being written is about how can we survive and be successful as opposed to being faithful. To be faithful, means doing what we believe God is calling us to do and trusting God with the outcome. We must remember that the church exists because God wants it to exist. We are called to be the church and to follow Jesus to the best of our ability, letting the chips fall where they may and trusting God with the results. The results may be in the next generation, in the next movement or in the next reformation. The point is that we are here to glorify God, and not the other way around. This is the old issue of, "What if you gained the whole world and lost your soul – what have you really gained?"

We are called to a ministry of reconciliation reflecting that through Christ, we have been reconciled to God. Sadly, over time, the body of Christ, a denomination or a local church can experience alienation to the point of division. These divisions do not reflect the witness to Christ that the world needs. It is important for each of us as members of the body of Christ to take seriously our role to reach out and encourage opportunities for reconciliation. We need to remember the spirit of the 17th century Puritan, Richard Baxter who wrote: In things necessary, unity; in things doubtful, liberty; in all things charity.

Count the Cost

Following Jesus involves costs. This kind of suffering occurs when we choose to follow Jesus into the suffering world. A long time friend Z. Holler, a retired Presbyterian minister often says, 'Because I speak out about peace and justice; truth and reconciliation, I often feel like the guy that laid a turd in the punch bowl." As a result people don't want to hear what he has to say. So he realizes that by choices he has made he may not be invited to certain events. This is why we need so much the support of other brothers and sisters. Without it, we can become so isolated.

It is interesting how everybody loved Thomas Merton when he wrote *New Seeds of Contemplation,* but people thought he was "going off his rocker" when he started talking about nuclear weapons, war and peace, poverty and racism. Everyone loved Henri Nouwen when he wrote The Wounded Healer, but when he started to talk about Latin America and the handicapped in North America, he lost some of his followers. We are talking about moving to a more fully integrated Christian life where we are free no matter where we find ourselves. We are to follow Jesus.

When Jesus calls us, he reminds us to count the cost. As it says in Luke's gospel, we must be prepared to take up our cross daily. In our sufferings, we experience what it means to die to the false self in order to live the true life that God intends. Often, when we experience the pain of suffering, we are forced to confront our own weakness and through our weakness, as Paul says, we experience God's strength.

As we walk with those who are suffering the pains of the world, we walk with them taking on their pain even as Christ takes on our pain. For example, simply taking the time to listening to someone affirms them as a person and allows them to see themselves as valuable in the eyes of God.

You will know them by their fruits

Jesus said it is by their fruits that you will know them. The Christian life is a life that is reflected in our actions. Often it is in our immediate families where some of our greatest challenges occur. Sometimes it is easier to love the neighbor half way around the world than it is to love the neighbor around the block or the family member in our own home. Close relationships inevitably carry with them emotional consequences that magnify the significance of our words and actions. The strength of our faith will be reflected in those close relationships.

In addition, Jesus challenges us to extend the circle of those close relationships beyond our usual definitions of family and friends. Peter Storey, a Methodist Bishop in South Africa has said, "That is why you cannot ask Jesus into your heart alone." He will ask, "Can I bring my friends?" You will look at His friends and they will consist of poor, marginalized and oppressed people and you will hesitate, but Jesus is clear, "Only if I can bring my friends."

Quotes from Gordon Cosby
We moderate and polish off the world's thinking, and name it Christian. The church embodies the upside-down

kingdom. *Whatever the world admires is probably not good, according to kingdom values. The church is always anti-empire.*

Jesus doesn't give us a deeper relationship with him apart from his body. Jesus does not come to us alone. Jesus can't, because Jesus already has a people, he has a body, he has a family. And when Jesus comes to us he always brings his family with him.

Notes:
What about this chapter spoke to you?
What difference could that make in your life?

Seven

Engaging the Powers

*"...those who lose their life for my sake, and
for the sake of the gospel, will save it."*

The Word
Jesus foretells his death and resurrection

Mark 8:34-37

He called the crowd with his disciples, and said to them, "If any want to become my followers, let them deny themselves and take up their cross and follow me.

For those who want to save their life will lose it, and those who lose their life for my sake, and for the sake of the gospel, will save it. For what will it profit them to gain the whole world and forfeit their life?

Indeed, what can they give in return for their life?

Be angry but do not sin.
See the corporate sin of man and know;
   we all participate in some way.
Give us the anger of Elijah;
   help us to see what would anger God.
Help us to hear the cries.
Call our renewed hearts into action.

Peace between good and evil;
   is an impossibility,
We are called to be warriors for Christ.
Let us follow His footsteps,
   let us not fear opposition.
Strengthen us,
   O, Holy Spirit.

Jane Murden (inspired by Charles Spurgeon)

Engaging the Powers

We tend to view our faith all too often through the lens of our socio-economic status. We tend to justify our position through scripture in order to keep things as they are.

Separation of church and state

I grew up in the South, in a county where there were three races: blacks, whites, and Native American Indians. I literally remember the theatre that I went to as a kid having three doors. Three separate doors. The whites went in downstairs, and the blacks and Indians went upstairs where they were separated in the balcony by a solid wall. I remember experiencing such a contradiction between the stories I heard in church and the way the same church people interacted with people of different races. We were supposed to love our neighbors, but our neighbors who were black and Indian were clearly second class neighbors. I felt like that really made the faith we were proclaiming hollow.

I remember hearing about the chief of police who was a member of my home church bringing a gun to church one Sunday and saying, "No nigger is coming to our church." He brought his gun to stop them. It was just so incongruous with what I was learning about following Christ. I wondered how people could live out of one set of values in one setting and then be living out of another set of values in another setting?

It is a compartmentalization that says church is over here and politics is over there. Bishop Tutu[6] says, "If Christianity is not political it's not Christian." You can certainly understand his saying that in a context where the laws were used to enforce racial separation in South Africa. This has always been an important issue for me because I feel that the faith we proclaim too often does not have authenticity. We have hollowed it out by compartmentalizing our faith and our politics.

In the extreme form of compartmentalizing we create a worldview that does not require us to ask questions or to participate in dialogue with the world. It's not unlike what happened in Germany during WWII when Hitler said to the church, "Ok, we want you to bless what we are doing, but if you're not going to do that, you must stick to saving souls." This led to the national church's support of Hitler's agenda.

We are taught separation of church and state at such a young age that it filters out into our church life. However, separation of church and state was never meant to separate morality from politics. The constitution says there shall be no law establishing or promoting religion. This was to prevent what happened in England - a national church. But some people use this notion of separation of church and state to try and separate out any moral argument that would interfere with their political direction. I don't think that the founding fathers intended to say that we should not have moral conversations about our laws and how we live as a nation. That's entirely different from saying the Presbyterian church will be the national church and tax funds will support it and everybody who wants to be anybody has to be a member. No other church can be established in the country. That's a totally different thing.

During the civil rights movement in this country, people on the liberal left tended to say that we as a nation should reflect the moral values that we claim. Indeed the civil rights movement grew out of the black church in the south. Then in the 80's and 90's people on the conservative right said that we should live out our moral values in our politics, but their theology has led them and the nation in a different direction. Thus, there is agreement between the left and the right that our moral values and religious values should inform our national policies. The question is: What is our theology? What do we believe and in what direction will that lead us?

It is important to remember our history in order to be clear about the purpose and the meaning of separation of church and state, i.e. what it was and what it isn't. For example, I remember when I was in seminary the Attorney General of NC at the time was Rufus Edmondson. He had served as a staff member to the Watergate committee under Sam Ervin. He talked about how he was personally against capital punishment, but it was his job as attorney general to carry out the laws of the state. Therefore, he could, in good conscience, support the execution of convicted criminals. It's understandable that the Attorney General of the state would be expected to carry out the laws of the state. What bothered me was that he was willing to give up his own moral position for the sake of maintaining his job. In other words, his argument was, well this is the law of the state and I as the attorney general must carry it out; however, if this is your moral position, how can you continue to be the attorney general? That's the issue.

The great leader of Protestantism, Martin Luther, had this idea of two kingdoms, the secular kingdom and the sacred kingdom. Today reformed Christians don't accept that separation. We believe that all of life is spiritual. We do not say

I'm going to operate under one set of rules in this kingdom and another set of rules in this other kingdom, which would allow me to be the hangman for the state and be the priest for the church and see no conflict. I believe what is moral is moral. If you find that the state is in conflict with what your faith teaches you, then you have to do as Old Testament prophets did: stand up and call the state to account and be prepared to accept the consequences.

Back in the days of slavery the church in the South said slavery is a political issue and therefore we shouldn't get involved in that. Well, certainly it was political, but it was also economic and it was also moral. And yet because of the economic pressures and the political pressures, many good, upstanding people did not address it as a moral issue in the South because many people in the church had vested interests that were both political and economic. They gave up the moral ground.

A relative of mine, Colonel Thomas Roderick Dew, was president of William and Mary College during the Civil War. He wrote a book justifying slavery based on scripture. He used the existence of slavery in the Bible to justify the system of slavery in the South. It is easy to take scripture out of context and have it justify the things that we are doing. In Paul's letters he refers to brothers and sisters in Christ that were in slavery. However, he did not call directly for an end to slavery. Only in the years since the civil rights movement have mainline churches acknowledged the ways in which the church has been complicit in maintaining racial barriers. The misuse of scripture to support our socio-economic interest continues to plague the church and its witness. We tend to view our faith all too often through the lens of our socio-economic status. We tend to justify our position through scripture in order to keep things as they are.

A Different Perspective

Let's look at this from a different perspective. Let's try to understand scripture from the point of view of people who are at the bottom, people who have been pushed out and marginalized. I have a friend who once said to me, "Usually when I hear the word justice, it means 'just us'." From this upside-down perspective we can hear the scriptures in a new way. When we finally get to the point of loving one another as brothers and sisters, we can no longer accept things as they are. We become dissatisfied, which leads to change.

This new way of hearing the scriptures is illustrated for me in the story of the laborers in the vineyard (Matthew 20:1-16). The landowner comes and hires laborers at the beginning of the day to go out and work in his vineyard. Then later in the day he hires some more people and again at the very end of the day he hires some more. Each laborer worked a different amount of time and probably at a different pace. When the landowner calls them in to be paid at the end of the day they are all paid the same wage. Many of the workers are upset, "It is not fair! Some of us have worked all day, what's the deal?"

I originally heard that story as a story about disgruntled workers who are never satisfied versus management because I had come from a family that had more of a management perspective. The problem, of course, was with labor. Now I see that story differently. It is really about the generosity of the landowner who paid all of the workers the same thing, which was what they needed, a day's wage. They needed a day's wage in order to make it. So he paid them a living wage; what they needed to live whether they had earned it or not. They all got what they needed, not what they deserved. That is the way God works with us. God gives us what we need, not what we deserve. Thanks be to God!

The point is that God's grace cannot be qualified. Our relationship with God is given to us as a gift through Jesus.

The free gift of God's grace to us frees us from justifying ourselves by anything that we have done. Rather the Christian life is a life lived in gratitude for what God has done. This also frees us from judging others, recognizing that if we, too, are judged we would all fall short. The ground is indeed level at the foot of the cross.

I remember a friend who doubted that a murderer who came to believe in Christ would not have to pay in some way after death. He believed that somehow this person would have to suffer after death for sins of this magnitude. But guess what...grace is grace. Christ's grace washes away all of our sins which supports my notion that when everybody gets to heaven they will see some other folks there that they think aren't deserving. They've messed up the neighborhood. What are these people doing here? But if we love our neighbors as ourselves, it will be heaven; if not, it will be hell.

Another story within the vineyard story is that it is a parable of going to heaven. Somebody could be a Christian all of their life and another person might come to Christ in mid-life and another person might come to know Christ right before death. The radical nature of the good news is that it is good news for all. "The circumcised and uncircumcised"; the in and the out group; the least and the last, the left out along with the first, the famous and the unfortunate, everybody gets the same inheritance. Everybody gets what they need in this life and the next. The good news is, "Thy kingdom come, thy will be done on earth as in heaven," to quote someone who never wrote a book.

How do we hear the gospel?

The point is we often miss some truths in scripture because we don't hear these passages from the standpoint of the least and the last. The challenge is to read scripture from the point of view of the poor and disenfranchised. How then do we improve our acoustics? It begins by being in relationship with the poor. We must be with the poor in order to be able to see and hear life from their vantage point.

It's just like that guy who said, "Usually when I hear the word justice it means 'just us.' He had a perspective on life born out of his experience of the institutions of our society not being a means of blessing him. The key is that wherever we are, we are to be concerned about the least, the last and the left out in order to be faithful to the One we are following. This transcends countries, labels, time and whatever other category we may use to divide people. We don't always do it well but I think there is a need to be sensitive to the least among us. It is a central teaching of our Christian faith.

So the whole business of improving our acoustics is that all to often we gravitate toward our comfort levels and hang with people that see things the way we see them and hear things the way we hear them. When what we need is to be able to stick with people and to encourage one another in seeing the things we don't see and hear the things we don't hear.

An African-American pastor, a friend of mine, who had served African-American congregations and mixed race congregations, told me that when people were asked what they first thought of when they thought of Moses, the African-Americans would say the Exodus and the Caucasian-Americans would say the Ten Commandments. Why? Perhaps it is because they were viewing life from different vantage points.

Recognizing those in power

As we turn to the discussion of how to engage with those in power within our communities, we have to recognize that all too often, we are the powers. We as mainline Christians in the United States of America are all too often the ones that hold the power. The "powers that be" in Greensboro, North Carolina, often are in church on Sunday morning. Therefore, engaging those powers means engaging those individuals. Often people we know. Often even ourselves.

The deeper we go in following Jesus the more we find ourselves in conflict with the world around us. Will we go along with wages that are too low to live on, with workers without healthcare, with environmental abuse and with taking advantage of other people and their circumstances for lower prices or to improve our stock positions? Or will we be willing to pay the price? Will we be willing to follow Jesus wherever he leads, whatever the cost? Will we be willing to confront those in power in our own community in order for change?

How do we deal with that conflict? All too often we legitimize it in some way in order to hold onto our comfort. Whether we are talking about politics or economics (and it sure is hard to separate those two) the tug of those things is very powerful when compared with our Christian moral teachings. For example in a democratic society the ability to make choices is at the heart of our freedoms. It is important to allow for people's choices while at the same time supporting people in making moral choices. The pull of our political and economic leanings that provide our comfort and "security" often threatens to overwhelm the call of Jesus to follow him. This is where we find ourselves torn between the safety and security of the status quo for those of us who are "blessed" and the uncertainty of where Jesus would lead us if we would just follow.

I often find that when someone becomes serious about their Christian faith they find themselves in some sort of conflict with their work environment. That really makes it tough. It is hard. I empathize. It's important when we find ourselves in these conflicts to connect with brothers and sisters in Christ in order to be faithful to the gospel. This brings us back to our central point that too often the church is made up socio-economically of people just like us. In order to better hear the gospel we need to hear from brothers and sisters who have experienced life from different vantage points. This then will help us in our struggle as we seek to be faithful to Jesus rather than to be swept along by the culture of the comfortable.

How did Christ engage the powers?

When we look at Christ and what he did when he walked here on earth, he challenged the powers of his day. He expects us to do the same as a part of His living body, the church. Christ engaged both the religious and political power structures of his day. He ate with sinners and tax collectors and the Pharisees were upset. He dialogued with the Pharisees and his own disciples were upset. He preached and taught in the temple and turned over the moneychangers' tables and the priests were upset. All of this was part of a movement that threatened to undo the status quo and the Romans were upset. Jesus wasn't on anybody's side but he was for everybody. This is a key to how he engaged the powers; he was not owned by or beholden to any group, but was for God and, therefore, concerned for all the people.

This can be a paradigm for the way Christians engage the powers today. It is important to recognize that no one group can fully represent all of God's intentions, hopes and dreams for this world. Therefore, we should never make the mistake of identifying the Christian faith as being solely represented by any one political group or religious movement. At the same time we as Christians must engage with these groups in order to participate in and influence the political process.

Jesus basically was calling the religious authorities back to the principles of their faith. He was not satisfied with the hollowness of their faith that had only the outward trappings. In that respect, he was like the Old Testament prophets. He was a prophet calling his people back to their roots saying look, it's not all about the outward trappings of the temple

115

and the sacrifices, but it is all about loving God and loving your neighbor. Jesus did that in word and in deeds, through His teachings, His preaching and also through His healings. Through His words and deeds He engaged the powers and yet didn't engage those powers in such a way that He became like them.

This is one of the great temptations. We are tempted to deal with the powers of this world on their own terms with the hope of being more effective. Jesus didn't do that. He calls us to be salt and light to the world but if we lose our distinctiveness then we no longer have any saving power to offer. It becomes just the same old worldly power game.

When we become engaged

One example in my life when I became engaged is when I participated in the Kmart protest in Greensboro. We were trying to help encourage the management of Kmart to negotiate with a union for a labor contract. I really didn't want to get involved. But because of my personal relationship with some of the people who were pastors that were leading the protest, I didn't feel like I could just say, 'Well, good job, you guys, I'll stand over here and watch from the sidelines.' I felt that in order to really be a friend I had to be with them. That meant being with them on the front line, in the hope that God could use our willingness to stand with and for laboring people as a witness to God's justice.

I remember during this time one of our church members suggested we invite some of the labor folks to our church to speak. There was somebody in our church that was organizing it. And I said, 'Why don't you call the newspaper and see if they will publish the information and maybe some other folks will come.' When they contacted the newspaper they were told that it was too controversial to print. All of a sudden, I was in touch with the powers that be. I didn't know there was *anything* too controversial for a newspaper to print. This was just a little church meeting with some interesting speakers. We had invited the labor organizers to come and tell us what their concerns were and the newspaper wouldn't even print the notice of the meeting. Now, that put me in touch with the censorship that was going on. It also put me in touch with the fact that the media itself was tied into the establishment through its own financial interest. Kmart was a big advertiser.

They wouldn't print this little notice. What was the big deal? It put me in touch with the fact that if you push at a power group, they push back. When we feel that "push back" most people back away. But Christ never backed away. That's why he ended up where he did on the cross. That's why a lot of us still back away because we don't necessarily want to end up like Christ did. Dead. Crucified. It reminds us of Jesus' words, "Whoever would come after me must deny themselves and take up their cross." In engaging the powers, you better believe that the powers are going to want to hold on to the way things are.

The whole experience with the Kmart protest was not costly to me in any significant way. The worst thing I had to do was call my dad and explain to him what I had done. Someone else might have lost their job. For someone else it could have been very costly. For Jesus the temptation was to take the least costly way just as it is for all of us. You can just imagine the disciples when he began teaching them that he must suffer and die and the disciples were saying, 'No!! You can't do that, that's crazy!' And Jesus said, 'Get behind me Satan. Don't tempt me with that way because that's not the way.' His way was a way of self-sacrificing. He calls us to take up our cross, to deny ourselves and follow Him. Jesus was ultimately pointing to the way that God's kingdom would come in its fullness.

Free to make a stand

Over time God puts us in the place where there is nothing to lose. This most often happens gradually. As we grow in our dependence on God we are set free from the pull of the things of this world and therefore have less and less to lose as we seek to follow God's leading. Then we are free to make that stand when called upon. That's why there has to be a beginning. You don't typically go from being the CEO of a company and the next day stand up for wage abuse in front of Kmart. That happens occasionally but is very unusual. Take a step in the right direction and God will lead you. He is always calling.

It took Paul a while after his Damascus Road experience for anything to happen in his life. Those things do not happen overnight. There is a progression. Paul spent years wandering in his own wilderness being prepared for the ministry he would undertake. So part of engaging the powers is finding the freedom to respond to God's call.

Hold on just a minute

Another of my experiences in confronting the powers was when I went to the county commissioners meeting to protest against budget cuts for social programs. For the first 45 minutes the pro-budget cut side had the floor. We were all sitting there saying, "Man, what is going on?" Normally you would have someone pro and then con, someone for, someone against. But that was not happening. Finally this black woman stood up and said, 'Hold on just a minute,' in a loud voice. I would never have done that in that setting because I'm so used to the establishment working for me. She was not used to the establishment working for her and she was not going to wait any longer for her voice to be heard. It was an eye opening experience. To be with folks for whom the establishment doesn't work. It gave me a new and different perspective, to see that those in authority don't always do the right thing. I had grown up thinking that to a large degree, they did do the right thing.

Another example for me would be becoming involved with Bread for the World.[7] My involvement has not been costly in any sense. It has been an opportunity to engage the powers on behalf of the people who don't get to sit in a Congressperson's office. We who have some positions of power and influence in society can use our voice to speak on behalf of those who have no voice or opportunity for influence. There is a phrase in the Presbyterian Church USA Brief Statement of Faith that says: We listen to the voices of people long silenced.

Bread for the World is a good example of working within the system. But even there you can't really get something done unless you have the political pressure to do it. People will hear you and me and be real nice and say, 'Well, Frank, it's good to have you here and glad you're doing your part.' Then they go ahead and vote however they feel they are going to get political support for voting.

Another reason I like Bread for the World is that it is on the legitimate side of advocating for the poor. The organization informs and educates and tries to help people see things they may never even look at. If BFW was in a different, less legitimate format people would be less likely to pay attention. BFW provides what I would call an entry level activity so that people might be able to see and hear the poor without getting personally active in someone's life. It is stepping in the right direction.

Addicted to the things of this world

In our society when we think of addictions we typically think of addictions to drugs and alcohol. I remember a powerful incident that occurred at our church one evening when a young man came in drunk and wanted to go into detox. I couldn't get him in that night so I told him, 'They will have a bed available tomorrow morning. I'll put you up at the Greensboro Inn and I'll come back and pick you up tomorrow morning at 8:30." When I arrived there the next morning and knocked on the door, he was not there. He was gone. Later that day, I saw him on Tate Street and I was so angry I pulled the car over and I rolled down the window and I said, "Hey, I missed you this morning. Where were you?" He held up this big beer in a brown paper bag and said, "You know where I was." It was like a ball and chain. It was as though he could not get away from his addiction.

A more common addiction in our society is that we are addicted to having more and more things and like any addiction these things never fully satisfy. We are always requiring the next fix. The problem is this desire to have more of the things we want is addictive. The good life is seen as a life of prosperity and is an essential part of the American dream. A life so defined is hostile to the ways of Jesus. He said, "It is easier for a camel to go through the eye of a needle than for the rich to enter the kingdom of God." That is the problem.

But we live in denial, which is classic addictive behavior. We instinctively try to explain how we're not really rich. And you have a point, if, like me, you belong to one of the middle-income brackets; which includes most of us in the industrialized north. However, compared to 99% of history's human population, or even compared to the vast majority of the people today, we are rich indeed. In any case none of us have to be wealthy to covet wealth. It is the love of wealth, not the amount of wealth that starves a soul and our culture fosters that love.

The soul takers

Let me tell you a great story. Two women were out plowing in a field. All of a sudden the plow gets stuck on something. They think it's a rock and so they move the plow and start digging. Instead of a rock they find the top of a treasure chest. They think, what in the world is this? They dig a little more and they open the treasure chest, finding it full of gold coins. They draw back. About that time four guys walk up and say, "What are you women doing?" The women gasp and say, "It's the soul takers." They run away.

The guys look down and they say, "Oh my gosh, look at this." Two of the guys say, "Why don't you two go into town and get us some lunch while we finish digging up the treasure chest. Then we will be ready to go by the time you get back." They agree and go into town. On the way to town they figure out that if they only had to split the treasure two ways they would get twice as much money. And so they decide to put some poison in the food for lunch.

In the meantime the other two men are digging and they decide if they only had to split the coins two ways they would get a lot more. They planned to lie in wait when the other two came back, ambush and kill them. So sure enough the two men come back with lunch and the other two lie in wait and they kill them and eat the lunch.

The women come back and find the four men lying dead around the treasure chest and the women exclaim, "The soul takers!"

What strikes me about that story is that I have often thought that money was neutral. It is just a tool. This story implies there is some kind of power in money or wealth. The power is in what we think wealth can do. Therefore, we have given it power over our lives. That power is fostered by society because people believe that wealth can buy them position, relationships and happiness.

Building bigger barns

To deal with any addiction we must put something in its place. We must become rich toward God. This is the point of Jesus' parable of the rich fool. Jesus said "Take care! Be on your guard against all kinds of greed for one's life does not consist in the abundance of possessions." Then he told them a parable: "The land of a rich man produced abundantly. And he thought to himself, 'What should I do, for I have no place to store my crops?' Then he said, 'I will do this: I will pull down my barns and build larger ones and there I will store all my grain and my goods. And I will say to my soul, 'Soul, you have ample goods laid up for many years; relax, eat, drink, be merry.' But God said to him, 'You fool! This very night your life is being demanded of you. And the things you have prepared, whose will they be?' So it is with those who store up treasures for themselves but are not rich toward God (Luke 12:15-21). This parable is probably not a frequent source of sermon material in our well-to-do congregations. It is, however, clearly an important text reminding us of the dangers of wealth in terms of our spiritual lives.

The end of the story, about building bigger barns, calls us to become rich toward God. How do we do that? Trust in God. Put God's kingdom first. Share what we have with those in need. Let go in order to let God be God in our lives. The perfect way is when our will and our desire is that God's will be done; that our requests are God's will. In the Lord's prayer the model is "Thy kingdom come, Thy will be done on earth as it is in heaven. Give us today what we need for today. Forgive us..." and so, we pray that our prayers will be God's will. Help me to want what you want, Lord.

Engaging God's kingdom

A part of engaging the powers in our culture is recognizing that many of us who are mainline Christians are a part of the world's power structure. The challenge is to be able to disengage from the values of the world's power structure while at the same time using our positions and voices to speak to the power structure and engage with it. We are freed by Christ from the values of this world, but we are also in this world where we can be used for God's glory and will.

We can be a voice for the poor; we can go and talk to our congressperson. At the same time we have to be careful that we don't sell out in order to have more impact.

We remember that James and John were tempted to seek positions of power and privilege instead of opportunities for service when they asked Jesus if they could sit one on his right hand and one on his left hand in his kingdom. But Jesus reminded them that to be great in God's kingdom means becoming a servant of all. As followers of Jesus when we engage the powers of this world we must be careful to reflect the values of God's kingdom and not get caught up in the ways of the world.

Quotes from Gordon Cosby

If a person is addicted to power, how can he receive a helpless baby and a crucified man into their lives?

We often don't let ourselves make the connection between our favored position and the cost that millions are paying for our standard of living.

We feel that we have a right to our privileges which is another way of saying that we have a right to be better than others.

There must be an inner movement deep within our souls toward the victims on life's road.

Notes:
What about this chapter spoke to you?
What difference could that make in your life?

Jesus Washes Our Feet

"...wash one another's feet.'

The Word
Jesus Washes His Disciples Feet

John 13:3-5,8,14-15

Jesus, knowing that the Father had given all things into his hands, and that he had come from God and was going to God, got up from the table, took off his outer robe, and tied a towel around himself. Then he poured water into a basin and began to wash the disciples' feet and to wipe them with the towel that was tied around him.

"Unless I wash you, you have no share with me."

So if I, your Lord and Teacher, have washed your feet, you also ought to wash one another's feet. For I have set you an example, that you also should do as I have done to you.

The apostles were people just like us with the same weakness and temptations as we have. Yet we are all 'saints' called by grace and sanctified by God's spirit. We have the same light that they had and the same grace accessible to us. The apostles lived with Jesus, they lived for Jesus and they grew like Jesus. They have left us their memories in written form for us to follow. Let us live by the same Spirit as they did. And follow in Christ's footsteps as they did. Let us stay courageous and be heartened by all they did and all those since them. Let us keep the faith.

paraphrased from "Morning and Evening: Daily Readings"
by Charles Spurgeon

---------- **Eight** ----------

Jesus Washes Our Feet

Then I looked again at all the injustice that goes on in this world. The oppressed were crying, and no one would help them. No one would help them, because their oppressors had power on their side. Ecclesiastes 4:1

Model and motivation

Jesus is not only our model for showing us the way, but also our motivation. He gave himself for us. In Jesus we see how we are to live and why we are to live. The term often used to express Jesus' style of leadership is servant leadership; that term seems incongruous; a servant and a leader. We don't think of those together because most of our leaders have many servants. So how can we put servant and leader together? It seems paradoxical.

The story of Jesus washing the feet of the disciples is such a great example of servant leadership because he shows them what to do and he does it for them. He models and then he provides the motivation for them to carry out service to others. One of the hardest concepts for most Christians is the very same issue that Peter had. We have a hard time letting Jesus serve us. We feel like we should serve Jesus.

Our first impulse is often to want to serve others before we have been served. Yet the message of this scripture reading is that we can only serve out of the reservoir of the recognition that we have first been served by Jesus, just as we can only forgive others as we first understand that we have been forgiven. In this way we have the well of spiritual grace from which to draw service and forgiveness for others. It is the difference between serving and forgiving out of our own ego versus serving and forgiving based on Christ.

Without Christ washing us first, our serving and for-giving others is hollow. It can even be a way of keeping others in an inferior position. It then could become all about us and how great we are. Oh, Reverend Dew, he is just soooo wonderful…he did this and this…well, if it's only about me, how has the other person been lifted up?

Forgiveness is at the heart of the cleansing, the washing of our feet. Maybe the disciples had dirty feet, but deeper than that, what's going on? Christ says, "If I have not washed you, then you have no part in me." This puts forgiveness at the heart of the gospel. It is the heart of the good news. I'm not ok and you're not ok, but Jesus said that's ok. We are forgiven.

Then the Christian life becomes one of living in response to that good news. We serve in gratitude and thanksgiving, rather than trying to live up to some standard which we can never reach, because we always screw up, just as the dis-ciples did. Jesus washes their feet and then tells them to do to others that which he has done for them. In other words, you've been forgiven, now go forgive and serve others.

What got Jesus in the most trouble? Forgiving sins. "Who gave you the authority to forgive sins? This is blasphemy!" came the cry from the religious authorities. The big deal, of course, was that the religious authorities had a whole system for forgiveness of sins; a whole system that they controlled, namely the temple sacrifices. The people were dependent on this system of granting forgiveness and it was also a great moneymaker for the religious establishment. But Jesus said, pointing to the Old Testament prophets: look, I'm not interested in your sacrificial lambs. I am your sacrificial lamb. Thus Christ messed up the whole system. No wonder they wanted to kill him.

One of my favorite stories is about a statue in a German cathedral that was found at the end of World War II. It was a statue of Jesus with the hands broken off. Everyone said, "Oh, let's repair the hands." That was their first impulse. But then they said, "No; we are the hands, we must be Christ's hands now." And so they left the statue the way it was. Therefore, as Christ serves us forgiveness, he shows us the way in word and in deed. He heals our brokenness and he feeds our souls. He gives us strength to do what we can only do through Him. We become his hands.

Turning things upside down

As Jesus often does he turns things upside down. He says in order to be great in the kingdom you must be a servant. Jesus' example is the way that we approach the Christian life. We lead by serving others. We serve at the point of our giftedness. In other words, I am not going to serve by leading singing because I've never been accused of being a good singer. If anyone has to depend on me to lead the singing, they're in big trouble. Nor am I gifted in being able to manage the financial end of things. That is not my gift. This is the point at which we trust God to call others who are gifted in the ways that are needed.

This can be a great experience in trusting in God. We say to the Lord that we need some help with music or we need someone to be our treasurer or to work with the youth or whatever. And then we can see God at work as we see people called to do these jobs. It is a real experience in trusting God and letting God work. In the waiting and trusting, we are often uncomfortable. We want to rush in and fix things, sometimes prematurely, by trying to jam someone into a role that they really are not gifted in or called to do. The idea is that we are called to serve at the point of our giftedness. Sometimes those gifts may be readily apparent and sometimes they show up surprisingly. We may find ourselves saying, "Oh, I didn't know you could do that."

Sometimes we just have to show up and in the midst of a meeting we come to realize why we are there and what role we are to fill. All of a sudden during a meeting we realize 'ah ha,' that's why I'm here. Sometimes God lets us know when we have helped or made a significant contribution. We can see that a decision would not have moved in a certain way if we had not been there. It is usually not what we were planning or had in mind, but there it is. And there is a gentle, warm response inside that says inwardly, that's why I'm here. Sometimes it takes more time than other times. Sometimes it can happen in a snap of a second and sometimes you can carry on for years not knowing why you are in a certain place. Underlying all of this is not that God *might* have a plan; it is that God *does* have a plan and our part is to find our place in that plan and participate.

We will not always know how we have contributed to a situation, but God does give us those special nuggets of affirmation so we won't just give up. We will never get it completely. We are just like the disciples. Jesus asked his disciples after he told a parable, 'Do you get it?' Christ realized they didn't get it and many times we don't either.

Taken, Blessed, Broken and Given
Forgiveness is so necessary because we are always falling short. And as we continue to follow we get it along the way. In the process of following we have the experience

of being cared for. The disciples wanted to be followers and we want to be followers. God honors that desire. To see the world with Christ's perspective; to hear with His ears and His heart, is an upside down perspective or perhaps more accurately His is the right side up.

It's not about our simply getting it; it is about our desire to follow Him. The best way of expressing what it means to be a Christian is to be a follower of Jesus: to try to follow in His way, to do the things that he did, to care about the things that he cared about. Putting on the mind of Christ is really what it means to be a servant leader. It just might be that the One through whom all things were created, namely, the Word, might know a little more than we do. He is the ultimate realist. It is more blessed to give than to receive. That's God's economy. That is the way the world works best. To be great in God's kingdom is to serve all.

People often say that the way of Jesus is just not realistic. From the perspective of the world as it is, war, weapons and wealth are the source of our security. Where has this kind of thinking gotten us? Does the world seem to reflect God's dream for the world? Have we turned our swords into plowshares? There is a need for a conversion of our perspective from the value system of the world to the value system of God's kingdom. We continue to forget that it is the meek that will inherit the earth.

In 1989 The Church of the Saviour started the Servant Leadership School. They invited about five groups from around the country to come to Washington for some training to develop servant leadership schools back in their locale. I was part of this first group that was trained.

I was going up there with the notion that we were going to learn servant leadership as a technique. I thought I would get a notebook with tabs and we were going to learn how to turn into a servant leader. Lo and behold, Henri Nouwen led the course! What he used as the basis for that weekend was his draft text, which later became the now well-renowned book, *Life of the Beloved*. I realized that servant leadership is not a technique, but an attitude. It is putting on the mind of Christ. It's the inward transformation that allows us to see the world right side up.

In *Life of the Beloved*, Nouwen takes the words of institution of the Lord's supper.. taken, blessed, broken and given.. and says that this is really the model of Jesus' life. He was taken (called or chosen), blessed by God, broken and then given for the sake of the world. Therein is our model. How then are we taken, chosen or called? How are we blessed? How are we broken? How are we given for the sake of the world? We are called to follow in that way. Our motivation is that Christ has been taken, blessed, broken and given for each of us, and we, as His followers, are to go and do the same.

Blessing each other

One of my favorite memories from the weekend is the story Henri told toward the end about one of the guys at the L'Arche[8] community who kept asking Henri to bless him. We're not used to blessing each other in the Protestant life. We aren't even used to a priest giving us a blessing. But this was a big thing in this setting and so Henri kept saying to this guy that he would get around to it. The guy kept asking him for a blessing. He kept pestering Henri until Henri finally gave him a blessing.

As he told this story about blessing that guy in that L'Arche community, he also called each one of us up for a blessing. Well, I wasn't all that accustomed to that. So I went up there and I was just amazing because it seemed that he had come to know each of us over the course of the weekend and he had something personal to say to each person. I remember he said to me, "Hold on to your calling."

Many times since then, when I get disappointed or disgusted or frustrated or maybe even tempted to do something else, I remember his blessing. The memory is a great encouragement to continue to hold onto the calling that God has given to me. I guess I heard in that blessing: Don't let go of what you've been called to do. Press on.

I like the blessing because I think it goes back to the idea that we can bless each other. Christ called us to do that, to bless each other. Blessings from other fellow Christians refresh us. When we are tired, we need to be refreshed. We can become refreshed by reading the Word, by blessing others and receiving blessings. This is for the priesthood of all believers, not just for ministers and/or priests. Ministers and priests do not have blessings cornered. Christ said, "Now, as my followers you do this, what I have done for you." This blessing is a part of the abundant life.

When we are refreshed, we see things more clearly. We hear things that we might not have heard before. If we do not receive blessings and affirmations it is easier to fall back into the "normal" culture. It reminds us, just like communion is a reminder that we are called to a holy life. Do this, remembering me.

Quotes from Gordon Cosby
Gratitude is openness and receptivity to 'is-ness'. Much of our energies are spent resisting what has happened to us.

What we resist remains within us as unassimilated experience.

A human being is not fully alive until he knows the freedom that comes from love.

137

Notes:
What about this chapter spoke to you?
What difference could that make in your life?

Jesus Calms Our Storms

*"Who then is this, that even the wind
and the sea obey him?"*

The Word
Jesus calms the storm

Mark 4:35-41

On that day, when evening had come, he said to them, "Let us go across to the other side." And leaving the crowd behind, they took him with them in the boat, just as he was. Other boats were with him.

A great windstorm arose, and the waves beat into the boat, so that the boat was already being swamped. But he was in the stern, asleep on the cushion; and they woke him up and said to him, "Teacher, do you not care that we are perishing?"

He woke up and rebuked the wind, and said to the sea, "Peace! Be still!" Then the wind ceased, and there was a dead calm.

He said to them, "Why are you afraid? Have you still no faith?" And they were filled with great awe and said to one another, "Who then is this, that even the wind and the sea obey him?"

A Song of Praise

I waited patiently for the Lord's help;
Then he listened to me and heard my cry.
He pulled me out of a dangerous pit,
Out of the deadly quicksand.
He set me safely on a rock and made me secure.
He taught me to sing a new song,
A song of praise to our God.
Many who see this will take warning and
Will put their trust in the Lord...
You have given me ears to hear you,
And so I answered, "Here I am;
My devotion to you is recorded in your book.
How I love to do your will, my God!

Psalms 40:1-3;6-8

Jesus Calms Our Storms

*We look to Christ again as our model and motivation to see
what he did with his authority. Certainly one of the things
he did was to reach out to the poor and the left out, the least
and the last of his society. He became their friend. He lived
among them and advocated for them.*

Scripture fulfilled

The story of Jesus calming the storm from the book of
Mark is one of my favorite passages because it illus-
trates the many layers of meaning in scripture. "On that day
when evening had come Christ said to his disciples, 'Let us
go across to the other side.' And leaving the crowd behind
they took Him with them into the boat. A great windstorm
arose and waves beat into the boat so that the boat was being
swamped. But Jesus was in the stern asleep on a cushion.
They woke Him up and said to Him, 'Teacher do you not
care we are perishing?' He woke up and rebuked the wind
and the waves and said, 'Peace be still.' Then the wind ceased
and there was a dead calm. He said to them, 'Why are you
afraid? Where is your faith?' And they were amazed and said

to one another, 'Who is this, that even the wind and the sea obey Him?'" (Mark 4:35-41)

One of the really interesting things is that this story seems to parallel Psalms 107:23-32. This scripture passage reads as follows: "Some went down to the sea in ships, doing business on the mighty waters; they saw the deeds of the Lord, His wondrous works in the deep; He commanded and raised the stormy wind which lifted up the waves of the sea. They mounted up to heaven, they went down to the depths; their courage melted away in their calamity. They reeled and staggered like drunkards and were at their wits end. Then they cried to the Lord in their trouble and he brought them out of their distress; he made the storm be still and the waves of the sea were hushed. Then they were glad because they had quiet and he brought them to their desired haven. Let them thank the Lord for his steadfast love, for his wondrous works to human kind. Let them extol him in the congregation of the people and praise him in the assembly of the elders."

This Psalm certainly was a part of Jesus' scripture and was probably part of the background of the story of the calming of the storm. The Lord who calmed the waters in the Psalm was seen in the life and work of Jesus. And so we ask the question, "Who is this, that even the wind and the sea obey Him?" One of the most important questions we can answer is, "Who is Jesus?" This story ends with that question. The story doesn't literally answer that question, but it does provide an answer.

This story is such a great example of the way I think of scripture. One of the biggest issues in the church today is the question of how we understand scripture. Someone has said that to take the Bible literally is not to take it seriously. Taking the Bible literally limits our ability to hear the many aspects of a given passage. How often have you read scripture that was familiar and yet because you were in a different place in your life you heard it in a new and different way?

To use another analogy, scripture is like a many-faceted precious stone. When you turn it in the light you see facets of the stone that you did not see initially. Likewise, there are many facets to this story.

Where will we find Christ?

Let's begin by looking at the question of the identity of Jesus because a person's identity has everything to do with how we respond to them. For example, when my drain is stopped up at home and a guy comes to the door wearing a white lab coat and a stethoscope, I'm impressed but he is not going to be able to help me with my stopped-up drain. Likewise if I'm lying in a hospital bed and somebody comes in with a tool belt and a plumber's friend and says, "Rev. Dew, you're scheduled for surgery," I would be getting a little nervous. So a person's identity has a lot to do with how we respond to them. And so we are asking, "Who is this, that even the wind and the sea obey Him?"

Now going back to the beginning of the story, Jesus and His disciples are going to the other side of the lake. Typically in the gospels the other side means the Gentile areas. So they are going to the other side and this storm comes up. Now on one level we all can appreciate the vulnerability of being out on a lake in the midst of a storm, a boat being swamped and calling out for help. They were looking for help from Jesus, and where was he? Asleep!

It drives me nuts when someone can sleep in the midst of chaos. How can you be sleeping! Don't you see what is going on? I could never do that, although part of me wishes I could. So anyway…they are frantic and they are saying, "Master, don't you even care we are about to drown here? Come on!" Then Jesus gets up and rebukes the wind, and the waves cease and there is a calm. And he asks them, "Where is your faith?" Where is your faith? Where is your trust in God? Don't you believe that God is in control and has a plan

147

and a purpose? They are terrified and amazed at the same time. And they say, "Who is this?"

One facet of this story is on the literal level of being caught in a storm. Another facet would be being caught in one of those storms that happen in the pits of our stomach when we are dealing with family problems, loss of a job, loss of a place to stay, illness or a death. All of those are storms in our lives when we might ask: Where is Jesus? And we do ask: Where is Jesus? Doesn't He care? Doesn't He know what I'm going through?

Who is Jesus?

Christ's question to us is: Don't you have faith? Don't you have faith to know that I am with you even in the midst of your difficulties? Christ does not insulate us from the hurts of the world, but he does go with us through them. This story is a reminder to us that whenever we find ourselves in the midst of a storm, Jesus is right there in the boat with us and through faith in Him our storms can be calmed.

One of the earliest symbols of the church was a boat. In this story Jesus' followers are in the boat, in the midst of a storm, facing persecution. Where is Jesus? Doesn't He care what they are going through? And where was He? He was right there with them, in the boat. Where is He in the midst of our storms? He is right here with us.

The story doesn't provide a literal answer to Jesus' identity, but the story does tell us that Jesus is the one who has the power to command even the wind and the waves. We can think back to the prologue of John's gospel where it says: "In the beginning was the Word and the Word was with God and the Word was God and not anything was made that was made except through Him." He is the Lord. And because He has the authority to command the wind and the waves, He is Lord. The Lord is the name that is applied to Jesus more than any other in the New Testament. In Jesus we see God's inclusivity offered to all in the particular- that is the person of Jesus. Because He is Lord, He is also our Savior, the one who can save us. He is the one who has the power to save.

The story never literally says that Jesus is Lord and Savior. What does a literalist do with this story? He's got a weatherman. If you look at the story literally it doesn't say anything about Lord and Savior. However, the story itself offers an analogy that shows Jesus acting as Lord and Savior in the midst of the storm. This storm analogy is a great example of how scripture can reveal so much of the light of God's truth if it is not limited to a literal reading.

Christ knew the Scriptures

If you find yourself in a desperate situation and you begin to say to yourself, be not afraid, you are remembering and repeating scripture. Jesus knew the Hebrew scriptures. He knew the Law, the Psalms and the Prophets. The gospel writers knew these same scriptures and they also knew who Jesus was as they looked back from the perspective of the resurrection. Jesus was the Messiah, the fulfillment of Hebrew scripture. The gospel accounts of Jesus were written in retrospect, like the conclusion of a good detective novel—all the plot lines and pieces of the puzzle came together in the end. The experience of the resurrection put the pieces together. At that point the gospel writers could say, remember when he said this and remember when he did that? It was just like what Isaiah said it would be and it was just like passages in the Psalms. The key thing for me is who the gospel writers understood Jesus to be rather than being limited to what he may have literally said or done.

Once we have answered this most important question of who Jesus is, we are ready to confront the reality of this primary relationship and our response to it. Is Christ just an exceptional social worker? Is He a controversial radical politician? Is He one of the great teachers of humanity? We find that even though He is all those things, He is even more. One of the confessions of our denomination is that Jesus came to show us what God is like and what human life is meant to be like. We can then affirm that Jesus is fully divine and fully human. We cannot fully express who Jesus is unless we put those two together. We need both the divine and human lens to bring into focus who Jesus is. Jesus shows us in human form what God intends for our lives.

When we understand that Jesus is Lord and Savior, then how do we respond to Him? What is the appropriate response? If He is the Lord and Savior of the world and of our individual hearts and souls, how shall we respond? How then can we live our lives in thankful, grateful response for what He has and is doing for us?

Christ's authority

Jesus' identity as Lord and Savior leads us to the issue of His authority in our lives. It's clear in the gospel accounts that Jesus taught as one who had authority unlike the other religious leaders of his day. What was that authority? Where did it come from? For example, when we think back to writing term papers in school it was important to have footnotes from authorities in order to justify our conclusions. On the other hand, Jesus didn't speak in a secondhand way trying to justify his teaching based on what others had said. Instead Jesus spoke directly out of His relationship with His heavenly Father (His Abba). Jesus did not have any footnotes, well, maybe one.

As followers of Christ we too can speak with this kind of authority based on our relationship with God through Christ. The question then arises about what we do with this kind of authority. We look to Christ again as our model and motivation to see what He did with His authority. Certainly one of the things He did was to reach out to the poor and the left out, the least and the last of His society. He became their friend. He lived among them and advocated for them. He had close personal relationships with the people the established society shunned, either with actual laws or indirectly though cultural taboos.

It reminds me of a time when we had a community meeting of various agencies and ministries that were serving the homeless and we were all talking about various problems we were facing. The man who ran the night shelter for the Urban Ministry at the time began to talk. He began to tell stories about individuals, using their names. It was like that old E.F. Hutton commercial: all of a sudden everybody was really listening to what he was saying because he was speaking with a kind of authority; firsthand knowledge. It wasn't out of a study. It wasn't out of a footnote from a survey. It was out of his personal experience; the authority that comes from firsthand knowledge. Then you are able to go to the "powers that be" and say, "Look, I have seen this, I know this from my own experience because I have been with them. I know them, I know their names, I know their faces, I know their stories."

Quotes from Gordon Cosby

Always when someone hurts you, there is a need in their life which needs ministering to, and as a Christian we ought to be more aware of their need than we are of our hurt.

The new birth does not impose on the personality something that is alien to it; rather, it brings into actuality, into fullness, that which was always there, those sensitive feelings, those yearnings, those tastes, that more tender dimension of our natures which somehow has always embarrassed us.

Notes:
What about this chapter spoke to you?
What difference could that make in your life?

Jesus Leads

"Feed my lambs, tend my sheep."

The Word
Jesus reinstates Peter

John 21:15-17

When they had finished breakfast, Jesus said to Simon Peter, "Simon son of John, do you love me more than these?" He said to him, "Yes, Lord; you know that I love you."

Jesus said to him, "Feed my lambs."

A second time he said to him, "Simon son of John, do you love me?" He said to him, "Yes, Lord; you know that I love you."

Jesus said to him, "Tend my sheep."

He said to him a third time, "Simon son of John, do you love me?" Peter felt hurt because he said to him the third time, "Do you love me?" And he said him, "Lord, you know everything; you know that I love you."

Jesus said to him, "Feed my sheep."

The Holy Spirit is constantly turning our eyes from self to Jesus. Do not listen to the impish doubt that comes in telling you that your sins are too great to be forgiven; that you don't have enough faith or any faith; that you are not repenting enough; that you will not be able to make it 'til the end; that you don't have the joy of God's children; that your grasp on Jesus is not strong enough. All these thoughts are about self, and we cannot find comfort or assurance by looking to the self. Christ is all in all. Therefore remember it is not your hold of Christ that saves you – it is Christ hold on you.; it is not your joy in Christ that save you – it is Christ; it is not even your faith in Christ, although that is the instrument- it is Christ's blood shed for you that has saved you. We will not find happiness by our prayers, our doings or our feelings; it is what Jesus is, not what we are, that gives joy and rest to the soul. Keep your eyes on Him; let His death, sufferings, merits, glories and intercessions be fresh on your mind morning and evening. Do not let your hopes and fears come between you and Jesus; follow after Him with all your strength and he will never fail you.

paraphrased from "Morning and Evening: Daily Readings by Charles Spurgeon

--------- Ten ---------

Jesus Leads

When we talk about 'improving the acoustics" what we are talking about is putting ourselves in places and with people that help us to hear more fully the good news of the gospel. To get in tune to the truth.

Entering the mission field

When Will Willimon was Dean of the Chapel at Duke University, he told a story about an African pastor who came to visit. He had just come from a large evangelistic mission that had involved baptizing many people back in Africa. There were so many people to baptize in the river that it got dark and they were worried about crocodiles. So he told the people to come back the next time and they would baptize the rest. He then traveled to North Carolina to preach at the Duke Chapel. During a conversation with Will, he asked, "Will, how many people have you baptized this year?" Will answered, 'Well, you know it's a university setting and maybe twelve or so in a year." The African pastor responded enthusiastically and with awe, "Oh, my goodness, I can't wait to go back home and tell everyone that I met a pastor who only baptized twelve people last year but he is still preaching the gospel! He hasn't given up!" He considered Will as being in a persecuted situation at Duke.

It is true. He is persecuted in the sense that the Christian message is so counter to the surrounding culture. But many would look at the pastor of Duke chapel, of all places, and think that he has arrived according to the religious, cultural standards in the USA. But actually just the opposite! He is still going after the sheep, even if it is only twelve. This is the same call that Jesus gave to Peter. Our calling is to be faithful, not necessarily successful. So Will rejoiced in the success of the African pastor and vice versa; both have lived faithfully with different results in their own context.

Looking at the closing story of John's gospel, "When they had finished breakfast Jesus said to Simon Peter, "Simon, son of John, do you love me more than these?" He said to him, "Yes, Lord, you know that I love you." Jesus said to him, "Feed my lambs." The second time he said to him, " Simon Peter, son of John, do you love me?" He said to him, "Yes, Lord, you know I love you." Jesus said to him, "Tend my sheep." He said to him the third time, "Simon, son of John, do you love me?" Peter felt hurt because he said to him the third time do you love me. And he said to him, "Lord, you know everything. You know that I love you." Jesus said to him, "Feed my sheep. Very truly I tell you when you were younger you used to fasten your own belt and go wherever you wished but when you grow old you will stretch out your hand and someone else will fasten the belt around you and take you where you do not wish to go." He said this to indicate the kind of death by which he would glorify God. After this he said to him, "Follow me."

Life as a doxology

The point of this story, indeed of all of life, is to glorify God. As I reflect on this scripture, I want to remove the part about Simon Peter getting old, but isn't that part of the point? We are human and even the way we pass on will glorify God. In our weakness we are able to point to God, but sometimes in our strength we are not willing to do so. Just as in the case of Jesus, at the point when the Roman Centurion recognized Him as the Son of God, Christ was being crucified. Jesus' glory was ironically on the cross. So in our times of trial and difficulty and going places we would rather not go, that may be when God is most evident to others in us. At that point we might not feel grace, love and mercy. But in our faithfulness we witness to others who are watching us suffer. Therefore God will be fully glorified as opposed to glorification of the individual.

In other words it's great to live for God when all the crabgrass is out of your yard and out of your life, and your kids are out of braces and everything is going great. But what is it to live for God in the midst of financial difficulty, in the midst of illness, in the midst of family difficulties, or in the midst of persecution? That's when it may be more evident that it is God who is sustaining us. I think that's why we are inspired by missionaries and others who are being persecuted for their Christianity. It is important for us to maintain close relationships with them and follow them because it is in such people that we can see faith so clearly. The darkness and hardships that are surrounding them provide a context that allows us to see the light of their faith. This then encourages us to be faithful in all circumstances.

We shall be created

God seems to work in spurts. The church is always being recreated. This renewal is always happening. When we look back over the history of the church, it is clear that the Spirit has been at work through cycles and recycles and various pendulum swings of reformation. And through all of these, people question what is really happening. In response to our questioning and our own limitations we come to realize that it is God who is at work through the Spirit in the church. We are also reminded in the Westminster Catechisms that the chief end of human beings is to glorify God and enjoy God forever. We sometimes act as if the chief end of God is to glorify us and our endeavors and our children and their endeavors.

A friend of mine says when someone asks him if he had a good day, he says, "Well, I don't really know." And what he means is I don't always know what's good for me. I know what I want but what I want is not always what is good for me. And of course the challenge is for us to grow to the point of sincerely wanting what God wants because that is what is good for us. God wants what is good for us and what is good for us is not always something that is measured as good by the world's standards.

The key to being servant leaders is that we are being led by God. As we go about the work of the church we need to constantly remind ourselves that the church does not belong to us, and that we are to be servants of God's will and intention. We are to express the life of the church in our lives as individual Christians in all facets of our days and nights. We are to be the body of Christ alive and at work in all the places of our lives.

What is our context for feeding and tending?

We are, in fact, in a missionary situation here in the United States. The mission field is right outside our door. Literally. We are always 'beginning' to figure this out in our time and place. That's the challenge. We must discern where God is leading us in our time and place and put that discernment into action. There are material needs even in the midst of plenty in this country. Ultimately, however, the solution to our societal problems lies in the recognition that our material wealth can never solve the problems of the human heart. The challenge of materialism is that we are tempted to believe that the problems we face are simply the product of the lack of material things and, therefore, the problems can be solved by simply adding more material things. This can be seen in individual as well as in institutional manifestations. For example, an individual landlord may decide not to repair or bring housing up to code in order to increase short-term profits. On a structural level the city may decide not to enforce the code in order not to offend wealthy taxpayers. Ultimately the individuals and the structures must be converted and renewed to a way of caring, especially for the least and the last among us.

Where do we begin? We begin by examining our own hearts, and as Jesus would say, by taking the log out of our own eye. We examine the ways in which we need to acknowledge our own sin before we begin talking about other people's sins. This then helps to put us in a place of humility and compassion rather than self-righteousness and contempt. Then we are able to speak about the speck that is in our neighbor's eye with love and mercy through Jesus Christ. We start with ourselves. In order for the church to offer an alternative to the world, we must be an alternative. If we are to be the salt and the light that Jesus spoke of, we cannot just simply reflect the values of the culture around us.

How many times have we heard someone say in a church board meeting, "Well, the church is a business and it's got to be run like a business"? What this often means is that the church should be run and operated based on the values of corporate America. If the church is to offer something different, we must first be something different and this means reflecting the counter-cultural values of the teachings of Jesus in our life together. This is not an easy road because so many of us have one foot in God's kingdom and one foot in corporate America and we experience ourselves being pulled in both directions. This is why it is so important for us to maintain our humility based on our need of God's grace, while at the same time keeping our eyes on Jesus as our model and motivation. The mission field in our context is at the water cooler at work or in the corporate boardroom where we have the opportunity to witness to the values of Jesus and encourage others to do the same. The idea is that the church is intended to be about transforming the world rather than the church being transformed by the world.

Our guiding principle

Our orientation is toward the work of the kingdom which calls us to action and to follow Jesus. It also means being available to respond to God's call. Our orientation is to God's glory. It is like a field of corn: we till the soil, we plant seed, but only God can give the growth. We each have a unique job to perform in order to tend the fields faithfully. As pastors, teachers, doctors, businessmen and women, wives, husbands, daughters, sons, etc.—the roles that seem to be defined by society—are actually our fields where God wants us to work and tend.

We as servants need to be open and willing to hear God's call wherever that may lead us. It may not be what we had in mind. I have to say that there are numerous things we have already talked about; for example, starting a church from scratch that I never would have wanted to do. I was imagining an oak paneled office with a country club membership at the swim and racket club. Especially when I started out, if I could have seen 20 years out, I probably would have run away. All that work for what? I would have thought, that's really not for me. But the truth is it was and is for me.

Christ does lead and our calling is to follow. We are not to remake him in our image and that is a real challenge. We need to try to see as clearly as we can who Jesus is and what he is concerned about and follow Him as opposed to remaking Jesus in our image.

When I was watching the news recently, the point was made that many churches today seem to be formed around what people want from their faith; whereas, classically religion has meant that a people disciple themselves to a teacher in order to reflect more and more the teachings of the Master. For us as Christians, Jesus is the Master and we are called to follow His teachings and example.

Let's get angry

The main point in following Jesus is to be sure that we are not creating a "Jesus" in our own image, but rather that we are being made more and more in His image. I think the key to that is sticking with the Jesus of the Bible. We can come back to the Bible and ask: What did he say? What did he teach? What did he do? Because there is such a prejudice in our society against getting angry, we tend to overlook places in the Bible where Jesus does just that. For example, we all know the story about the turning over the tables in the temple, but what about when he calls people hypocrites and white washed tombs?

We think that getting angry is somehow wrong or bad. The real question is what we get angry about and how we express that anger. All too often we get angry about things that are trivial (someone misplaced my keys) and fail to get angry about things that are really important (thousands of people dying each day because of hunger). As followers of Jesus, the challenge is to be concerned about the things that He was concerned about, to let Him be our guide in order that we will be angry about things that matter and not end up majoring in minors.

When Christ was on earth he did get angry. Thus, there is a place for anger, but not a place for hate. We shy away from any anger because we are afraid of anger. Maybe we are stressed out or maybe it will cause us stress and we know that stress is bad for us. We need to accept that we will get angry and stressed about the same things that made Jesus angry and stressed. If we're not angry and stressed about some of the things that are going on, then something is wrong.

Is the goal in life just to be happy all the time? Is that a goal to strive for? I don't think that Jesus woke up every day and said I'm just going to try and be happy all day long, I'm just going to be content. I will take my Prozac and get along with everyone no matter what they say or do. Is the goal in life to try and make everyone else happy? Is that a goal to strive for? I don't think Jesus woke up every day and said I'm going to try and make everyone happy today. We need to watch out for this because the feeding and tending component of discipleship can become a "making people happy" activity. It is another pitfall that we need to be aware of and watch out for, another deception.

Listen to Him

When we talk about "improving the acoustics" what we are really talking about is putting ourselves in places and with people that help us to hear more fully the good news of the gospel. To get in tune to the truth. None of us by ourselves can hear or see all that we need to hear and see, but rather we need to be in places and with people who can help us to hear and help us to see the fullness of the gospel. All too often we gravitate toward our comfort levels and spend time with people who see things the way we see them and hear things the way we hear them. Instead what we need is to be able to be with people and to encourage one another in seeing the things we don't see and hearing the things we don't hear. We are reminded that Jesus called both Matthew, the tax collector, and Simon, the zealot, who was sworn to kill tax collectors. If Jesus expected these two to love each other and to follow Him, that must be what the kingdom looks like.

Finally, don't let the words of this book be the end for you. Rather let this book be the beginning of your journey of following Jesus; going to the places he went, being with the people he was with in order to hear His call for you afresh. Don't be tempted to think that simply by reading this book that you have done something. Let this book be an inspiration for your doing. Take a break from reading about servanthood. You've got the idea, now go out and serve. As Jesus said, "Feed my sheep. Tend my lambs."

Quotes from Gordon Cosby

To follow Jesus is to be with him. We don't tell Jesus where to go, he tells us where to go or shares with us where he is going.

Call can be summed up in two words: Follow me.

Every person that I meet has something of Christ to say to me that no one else in the world can say.

To accept, to know the love of Jesus Christ, is to see life as gift, to see it as grace, to see it as feast, as banquet, because Jesus Christ is the gift of God.

Notes:
What about this chapter spoke to you?
What difference could that make in your life?

End notes

1 The Church of the Saviour is located at 2025 Massachusetts Ave. NW, Washington D.C.

2 Alcoholics Anonymous is an organization that helps people with alcohol abuse.

3 Gordon Cosby is co-founder of Church of the Saviour in Washington, D.C.

4 Quaker is the popular name for the Society of Friends founded by George Fox.

5 Miriam's Place is a small group retreat center in Southeast Guilford County, N.C.

6 Bishop Tutu is the former archbishop of the Anglican church in South Africa.

7 Bread for the World is a nationwide Christian movement that seeks justice for the world's hungry people by lobbying our nation's decision makers.

8 L'Arche was founded by Jean Vanier as a community in France for the mentally handicapped and their helpers.

Possible Discussion Questions

Chapter 1

Who do you know that has been called by God? Can you name someone who is not in traditional ministry? Ask that person when they first perceived their calling and how they keep their momentum going.

Do you have a ministry? If so, what form did your ministry take in the past week?

How have you experienced call?

What aspect of call described in this chapter was most helpful to you?

In what ways have you responded or failed to respond to God's call?

Chapter 2

What ideas in this chapter were most helpful to you?

What do you need to strengthen your prayer life?

How would you describe the value of prayer to someone who doesn't pray?

Do you presently have a structure in existence for daily prayer? If not, what would it take to create that?

Chapter 3

How has being part of a Christian community enabled you to be faithful in following Jesus? To what extent does your community help you to resist the pull of culture?

What are examples of our culture's dominant values that are at odds with your own Christian walk?

What levels of community described in this chapter have you experienced? How would your community need to change to be more authentic?

List all the events of yesterday, from getting out of bed to returning to sleep, including as much as you can remember. Draw a circle that represents your waking life. Divide it into "pie slices" that indicate how you spend your time, refer-ring to yesterday's list. Are any slices there because you care what other people think of you? How large is the "slice" for being in community with other Christians?

How diverse is your community? To what extent do you have the opportunity to be with people with different backgrounds, ideas, attitudes, socio-economic levels, etc.?

In what ways has your community helped you in confirming a call?

Chapter 4

Which of the types of poverty described in this chapter have you experienced?

What possession would you find difficult to give up? Can you imagine "...not having ownership of anyone or anything?"

When have you noticed God "...pulling you to some new territory?" How did you respond?

How have your experiences or lack of experience with poverty affected your faith?

What experiences have you had with the poor? When have you responded to the opportunity for relationship and when have you resisted being involved? Why did you resist?

How could your Christian community be more directly involved with the least and the last?

Chapter 5

Can you relate to the authors love hate relationship with the church?

Have you ever made a decision in community?

What kind of worship setting do you find yourself drawn to?

Chapter 6

Do you find yourself compartmentalizing your life into different segments where you actually act different?

Have you ever experienced suffering due to your own bad choices?

Have you ever experienced isolation?

How is it sometimes harder to "be a Christian" in your own immediate family?

Chapter 7.

What does separation of church and state mean to you?

Why is it good to review our own history and the history of our church?

How can wealth be power?

How can wealth be weakness?

How could I change my vantage point and therefore attempt to improve my acoustics?

How did Christ engage the powers?

Have you ever challenged "the power that be" in any aspect of your life? If not, have you ever wanted to? If so, when and what happened?

What "things" are you addicted to and what could you put in their place? Do you know "...the freedom that comes from love?"

Gordon Crosby said, "There must be an inner movement deep within our souls toward the victims on life's road." Do you ever feel that movement? If not, what gets in the way of your feeling it? If so, which victims come to your mind?

Chapter 8.

Do you have an example of some one serving out of their own ego?

Do you have an example of someone serve out of Christ?

Do you think Christ was/is the ultimate realist?

Have you ever had that "aha, THAT's why I'm here" feeling that Frank describes? Have you ever realized it in retrospect?

Chapter 9.

Have you ever experienced Christ rebuking the storms of your life?

Have you ever considered memorizing some of the Psalms?

How can we tell who or what we give authority of our lives?

Will you consider taking the time to become a real friend to someone who is physically poor?

Remember a time when you have been hurt by another person. Can you now see that there was a need in that person's life that needed ministering to? Could you see it at the time? Were you more aware of your own hurt or the person's need?

Chapter 10

Where is your mission field?

Describe a trying time in your life when it was hard to remain faithful?

When is a time you've been a missionary for Christ in your everyday life?

Should the church be run like a business?

How would we like to remake Jesus into our own image?

Are you in tune to the good news of the gospel?

9 781613 796238